D0875941

DEMONSTRATION DEMOCRACY

MONOGRAPHS IN SOCIOLOGY

Editor:
Bernhardt Lieberman, University of Pittsburgh

AMITAI ETZIONI, Demonstration Democracy

Other volumes in preparation

DEMONSTRATION DEMOCRACY

AMITAI ETZIONI

Professor of Sociology, Columbia University
Director of Center for Policy Research

A policy-paper prepared for the
Task Force on Demonstrations, Protests, and Group Violence
of the President's National Commission on the Causes
and Prevention of Violence

Prepared under the auspices of the
Center for Policy Research.

GORDON AND BREACH, SCIENCE PUBLISHERS
New York · London · Paris

Copyright © 1970 by Gordon and Breach, Science Publishers, Inc.
150 Fifth Avenue, New York, N.Y. 10011

Library of Congress Catalog Card Number: 72-112346

Editorial Office for Great Britain:
    Gordon and Breach, Science Publishers Ltd.
    12 Bloomsbury Way
    London W.C.1, England

Editorial Office for France:
    Gordon & Breach
    7-9 rue Emile Dubois
    Paris 14e

Printed in the United States of America

677-02610

MONOGRAPHS IN SOCIOLOGY

INTRODUCTION

It is a pleasure to be able to publish Professor Etzioni's monograph, "Demonstration Democracy" as the first volume of the Gordon and Breach Series in Sociology. This series will consist of monographs, textbooks, and collections of papers, each designed to contribute to sociological thought. The monographs will report the results of insightful and valuable research efforts; the textbooks will summarize some meaningful, reasonably well-defined area of study; and the collections of papers will bring together previously unpublished papers, or papers that have either been previously unpublished or papers that have been previously published, but which need to be brought together in a single volume.

HGR
15 December, 1969

"For three-year old Michael, who just participated in his first demonstration"

PREFACE

Most Americans tend to view their society as well advanced, politically stable and not very violent, although sophisticated observers point out to Americans that violence is frequently present in this country. Presidential assassinations, lynchings, abuses of police powers, threats and violence against negroes and blacks, and the violence and shootings in the newly settled western territories in the 19th century and early 20th century all indicate that violence was and still is common in the United States. We will probably never be able to answer the question whether the United States is a violent country; such a simple, naïve question is obviously unanswerable. It seems safe to say that different nations are characterized by more and less violence; there are some nations that exhibit more incidence of violence and others have less; placing the United States in its proper place along this continuum would be a costly and difficult piece of social research.

Whatever is the answer to this question, it is clear that many Americans, both politicians and ordinary citizens, were deeply disturbed by the demonstrations and violence of the mid-to-late 1960's. For many reasons Lyndon Johnson appointed the President's National Commission on the Causes and Prevention of Violence; the task of the Commission was clear, to help us gain an understanding and to help us prevent the commission of violent acts.

One of the subgroups of the Commission, the Task Force on Demonstrations, Protests and Group Violence, asked Professor Etzioni to examine the demonstrations by students, blacks, and other groups, to contribute to our understanding of them, and hopefully to offer recommendations to reduce

the violent aspects of demonstrations. This monograph is the
result of that request.

Professor Etzioni has done a number of things in this
monograph: he has examined reports of all demonstrations
reported in the New York Times and the Washington Post
for the one month period from September 16, 1968, to October
15, 1968, and he tells us something about these demonstrations; he has asserted clearly that he believes that demonstrations are likely to be a permanent feature of our political
system; and he offers some ideas based on his wisdom,
understanding, and sociological knowledge to show us how to
reduce the violent aspects of demonstrations.

Professor Etzioni's prose is lucid and incisive, and so I
would like to comment only on his statement that demonstrations are likely to continue to occur in the coming years.
Specifically, he states,

> "The rise in the number, frequency, scope and respecta-
> bility of demonstrations and their close link with tele-
> vision all suggest that demonstrations, as a major means
> through which protest can be expressed, are now and will
> remain part and parcel of the country's political processes
> and will not disappear when the war in Vietnam is over
> or the needs of the poor are met. For good or bad, they
> are now part of our system."

What Professor Etzioni seems to be saying is that at least
for the near future, the next ten years or so, demonstrations
will be a regular part of American politics, as they have been
for the past ten or so. Such a statement is well worth making,
and given Professor Etzioni's studies of contemporary society
one must consider his statement carefully. But one could
also imagine the next ten years in which the Vietnam War
ends; blacks and negroes are increasingly integrated into
American society; and the white middle-class students, who
are essentially a wealthy and privileged group, return to the
pursuit of their individual interests.

The next decade will give us information about these

issues. And, whether Professor Etzioni proves to be correct
or incorrect, he has posed some interesting questions in this
volume. His work will increase in value as the years pass and
we observe the course of events that Professor Etzioni has so
insightfully written about.

BERNHARDT LIEBERMAN
Pittsburgh, Pennsylvania,
December, 1969

HGR
December 15, 1969

TABLE OF CONTENTS

Introduction   1

I THE RISE OF DEMONSTRATION DEMOCRACY   3
   1. Frequency of demonstrations 3
   2. The number of participants 5
   3. The scope of participation 5
   4. Demonstrations as a political tool 6
   5. The violence of demonstrations 8
   6. The public view of demonstrations 9
   7. The role of television 12

II THE FUNCTIONS AND DYSFUNCTIONS OF
   DEMOCRATIC DEMONSTRATIONS   15
   1. An analytic orientation 15
   2. A digression into political theory 15
   3. Comparison of political means: Some functions of
      demonstrations 17
   4. The dysfunctions of demonstrations 20
      4.1 The "flattening" effect 20
      4.2 "Unrepresentative" representatives and "false"
         demonstrations 22
      4.3 Volatility 27
         a. Excessive restrictions 27
         b. Provocation by "by-standers" 29
         c. The police as a trigger 31
         d. Provocation by demonstrators 35
         e. The role of the media 39
   5. The cooptation argument: poor sociology .. 40
   6. Restoring civil disobedience to its special status .. 43

III RESPONSIVENESS: THE KEY FACTOR   45
    1. The intricate relationship of responsiveness to
      protest   46
    2. The role of leadership   49
    3. Participation 52

Appendix A: A demonstration Month—A list of 216 incidents 59

Appendix B: Methodological Notes   75

About the author   77

Achnowledgements   77

Appendix C: Commission statement on Group violence   79

DEMONSTRATION DEMOCRACY

INTRODUCTION

Each generation of Americans evolves its own procedures to sustain and reinforce democracy. While responsiveness to the needs of the people, the rule of the majority, and nonviolent changes of those in office characterize the assumptions underlying democratic procedures, the techniques used—such as town meetings and mass voting—differ from era to era.

Our generation is characterized by the evolution of new means of mass communication, notably television; by an increased mobilization of underprivileged groups in their demands for active participation in the political and allocative processes; and by increasingly complex bureaucratic structures—in government, education, religion, and other areas. *Demonstrations*, I shall show in detail below, are a particularly effective mode of political expression in an age of television, for underprivileged groups, and for prodding stalemated bureaucracies into taking necessary actions. Indeed, demonstrations are becoming part of the daily routine of our democracy and its most distinctive mark.

Today's American citizen has available a number of alternative forms of political action during the long periods between elections and in dealing with the numerous " private governments " not directly responsible to the electorate. In addition to writing letters to his representatives, submitting petitions, advertising in the press, and supporting organized pressure groups, a citizen may demonstrate to make known his views, especially his grievances, when expression through other means has brought no, or only inadequate, redress. In this sense, demonstrations are becoming for the citizen an avenue like strikes have become for the workers.

1

Like strikes, demonstrations—especially in this early stage of their evolution—entail one danger to which other forms of political expression are much less prone: they may escalate into obstructionism or violence. For a democracy to function effectively—indeed, for civil society to be sustained—it is essential that the modes of political expression be both non-violent *and* effective. That is, the inevitable differences of viewpoint, interest and belief *must* be worked out peacefully *and* the legitimate needs of all the member groups of the society must be taken into account. To suppress all demonstrations because they are a volatile means of expression would be both impossible under our present form of government and inconsistent with the basic tenets of the democratic system, in that it would deprive the citizens—especially the disadvantaged groups—of a potential political tool. And, it is a central conclusion of this policy-paper that *it is possible to increase the likelihood that demonstrations will remain peaceful*. The conditions under which protest is more likely to remain non-violent and the means for enhancing its peaceful nature are a major subject of our analysis.

In the following pages, we first elaborate and document, to some extent, our thesis that demonstrations are becoming an integral part of our democratic way of life (Section I, pp. 3-17). We then seek to specify the conditions under which some demonstrations become violent and explore ways in which the incidence of such violence can be greatly reduced (Section II, pp. 18-52). This paper next discusses the necessity for governmental responsiveness to legitimate, articulated needs; it is neither possible nor desirable to keep political expression peaceful if basic needs are continuously disregarded. However, as not all needs, not even all of those which are legitimate and articulated, can be fully answered, this paper closes with brief comments on the degree of responsiveness that is required if demonstrations—and, more broadly, the give-and-take in a democratic policy—are to remain peaceful, and the civil society is to be sustained (Section III, pp. 53-66).

THE RISE OF
DEMONSTRATION DEMOCRACY

1. *Frequency of demonstrations*

To test our impression that demonstrations have become daily occurrences in which large and varied segments of the public participate, one month was chosen at random, September 16, 1968 to October 15, 1968, and every incident of protest that was reported either in the *New York Times* or the *Washington Post* was recorded (with the exception of foreign protests, whose rate of frequency seems also to have increased). Of the 216 incidents reported as occurring in the United States, 70 took place in the New York metropolitan area, 33 in the Washington D.C. area, and 113 elsewhere in the country. Almost surely more incidents occurred than were reported, especially in parts of the country other than the two metropolitan areas as, of course, the newspapers we used are more likely to report incidents in their respective areas. Several limitations on the resources and time allowed for this study made it impossible to use newspapers from other parts of the country and to check the information reported in the press against other sources. We were also unable to compare the incidence of protests in the month studied with that in a comparable month five and/or ten years ago, to establish trends and changes.[1]

An occurrence was counted as an incident of protest if it involved uninstitutionalized political expression, especially taking to the streets or disrupting places of learning, worship, production, or political assembly. Initially, it was expected

[1] For additional limitations of the data and the rules which governed our categorization, see Appendix B.

3

that for the most part, the incidents would take the form of demonstrations in the narrow sense of organized marches down the street, similar to the way in which the anti-war, civil rights, and poor people expressed themselves. Actually, we found that many incidents involved other forms of demonstration—including prayer in the street (when St. Patrick's Cathedral in New York City closed its doors to a prayer against the war), welfare recipients causing a disturbance by presenting themselves *en masse* at a welfare center which had repeatedly ignored their demands, and student vandalism at New York University.

Webster defines a *demonstration* as " the act of making known or evident by visible or tangible means . . .," " a public display of group feeling." We adopted this definition. Demonstrations, thus, do not necessarily entail a march but are rather public acts designed to call attention to or express a position. The specific features of demonstrations—from the carrying of placards to obstructionalist acts—are intimately tied to this wish to make a position " visible or tangible," and it is this characteristic which distinguishes demonstrations from more routine forms of expression, such as regular participation in a town meeting or party convention. In this sense demonstrations are an extra-ordinary, not institutionalized, means of political expression.

By this definition, 216 demonstrations were reported in one month, or about seven per day. This figure is almost certainly a low one. As stated earlier, it is highly likely that some incidents which occurred in the metropolitan areas covered by the *New York Times* and the *Washington Post* went unreported, and this would hold to a much greater extent in other parts of the country. Moreover, incidents which were merely mentioned rather than described—e.g., " demonstrations also took place in nine other cities "—were not included in our count. Thus, there is no question that our estimate is a very conservative one, and that the conclusion that one kind of demonstration or another is a *daily* occurrence in contemporary America is justified.

2. *The number of participants*

The number of participants in demonstrations seems to be increasing and includes an increasingly large proportion of the members of society. Anti-war demonstrations in the United States, for example, are estimated to have grown almost continuously from the spring of 1965 to the spring of 1968, from approximately 100,000 participants a quarter of the year to about 280,000.[2] The student population, castigated in the nineteen-fifties as the " silent generation," produced at least 221 demonstrations in 101 colleges between January 1, and June 15, 1968, involving 38,911 participants, according to a study conducted by the National Student Association.

3. *The scope of participation*

Demonstrations are often viewed as the political tool of only a few dissident factions, such as students and Negroes. Actually, the number and variety of social groups resorting to this mechanism, at least on occasion, seem to be increasing. By this time, various middle-class groups as well as " respectable " professionals have demonstrated. Teachers have picketed schools in New York City.[3] " 300 doctors, nurses, researchers and others from the medical profession demonstrated against the war in Vietnam yesterday outside the Belleview Hospital compound."[4] Several hundred clergymen held a silent vigil next to the Pentagon on May 12, 1965. On several Sundays in September and October, 1968, parishioners demonstrated near Catholic churches in Washington, D.C. to protest sanctions against priests who did not support the Pope's edict against artificial birth control. Even the staffs of law enforcement agencies have not refrained from demonstrating. For instance, on October 1, 1968, one hundred " welfare patrolmen "

---

[2] Irving L. Horowitz, " The Struggle is the Message : An Analysis of Tactics, Trends and Tensions in the Anti-War Movement," a report prepared for the President's National Commission on the Causes and Prevention of Violence.

[3] *New York Times*, September 12, 1967.

[4] *New York Times*, January 5, 1967.

picketed New York City's Social Services Department at 250 Church Street.

Nor are the demonstrators of any particular political persuasion. Among those who have resorted to this mode of expression are students who demonstrated *for* Humphrey outside the San Francisco Civic Center Auditorium on October 15, 1968 (urging Senator Eugene J. McCarthy to support him), *against* the sit-in at Columbia University, *for* the war in Vietnam and *for* stricter enforcement of the law.

The net effect of this widening of the base of participation in demonstrations, we suggest, is the greater legitimation of this tool *that will lead in the future to even greater and wider and more varied participation in demonstrations*—i.e., an expansion of the scope of demonstration democracy.

This is not to suggest that all social groups demonstrate with equal frequency. Negroes and students do demonstrate much more often than other groups (See table 1). But members of such professional groups as teachers and social workers, who rarely took part in demonstrations a decade ago, now do so fairly frequently. And a very large segment of the anti-war demonstrators are white, middle-class citizens.

We suggest that "respectable" groups will demonstrate more frequently during the next decade, although the young and the under-classes are expected to maintain their special affinity for this type of political communication.

4. *Demonstrations as a political tool*

Only a few political tools are available to the average citizen between elections. If he becomes seriously aroused about one or more issues, he may be forced to wait to exercise his franchise as long as four years, and then he may cast only one vote to express his various positions—e.g., the war in Vietnam, law and order, social justice, etc. Between elections, a citizen can write to his Congressman, sign a petition, or add his name to a paid advertisement in a newspaper; his real options as a non-demonstrator are few.

Even though those who demonstrate are often depicted as a

TABLE 1

Participants in Protest in 216 incidents studied

Group		Group	
Negroes	37	Cuban Refugees	2
College Students	34	Catholic Priests	2
H. S. Students	27	University Employees	2
Anti-war	16	Mexican-Americans	1
Teachers	12	Church Members	1
Parents	12	" Welfare Patrolmen "	1
Hippies	11	Italian-American Students	1
Union Members	10	Mexican Grape Pickers	1
Catholics	9	Anti-HUAC	1
Community Residents	7	Cafeteria Workers	1
Anti-Wallace	7	Hospital Workers	1
Prisoners	6	Sanitation Workers	1
Welfare Recipients	5	Welfare Workers	1
Puerto Ricans	4	Professional Social Workers	1
School children	4	Housewives	1
Pro-Wallace	3	Policemen's Wives	1
Anti-Humphrey	2	" Voters "	1
Pro-War	2		

Note: 1) When the protesters had several relevant statuses, the one or two which seemed most pertinent to the particular demonstration was used as a basis for categorization.

2) When two groups participated in one demonstration, both were counted. Hence there are 228 groups listed.

small minority of the general population, the number of Americans who now feel the need for additional, more frequent, and more active modes of political expression appears to be approaching that of those who restrict themselves to the more sedate means mentioned above. It is reported, for instance, that the college demonstrations studied by the National Student Association drew only 2.7% of the full-time undergraduates at the schools studied. The civil rights movement has been described in a similar way; it has been pointed out that no more than a small fraction of the 20 million Negro-Americans have ever been mobilized into demonstrations. But the same is true for other forms of active political participation. While as many as 15% of those queried in a study[5] asserted that they were apt to display a button or

[5] Lester W. Milbraith, *Political Participation* (Chicago: Rand McNally, 1965), p. 19.

sticker, 13% might contact a public official, and 10% would make a monetary contribution to a political party or cause, only 4% to 5% said they were active in a party, or political campaign, which comes close in terms of levels of activation to those cited for demonstrations.[6] In short, taking into account all the preceding pieces of information, demonstrations—in terms of their numbers and range of participation—seem to be becoming a significant mode of political expression and a conventional, almost integral part of our democratic process.

5. *The violence of demonstrations*

There are basically three kinds of demonstrations: those which are entirely *non-violent (peaceful)* and legal, such as a march on Fifth Avenue following the issuance of a permit and in accord with its restrictions; *obstructionist* demonstrations, which entail, for example, blocking the traffic on a street, the entrance to a school, or the movement of construction equipment, and, as a rule, some degree of civil disobedience; and *violent*[7] demonstrations, which may include the throwing of missiles, fist fights, beatings, arson, and even shooting, and are clearly illegal.

Contrary to the impression which seems to prevail in many quarters, the majority of the demonstrations begin, are carried out, and end peacefully. Of the 216 incidents studied here, 134

[6] Note that the demonstration statistics are derived from data independently generated while the reports on other forms of political participation are based on self-reports, which seems to us likely to inflate the latter figures.

[7] By *violence* we mean an act of coercion in which physical force, or the threat to use it, is employed, to induce a person to act (or to refrain from acting) against his will, or to destroy or damage property. Other means of coercion such as economic sanctions or psychic deprivations, may be called—together with violent acts—brutalization, victimization or " violation " but are not referred to here as violence. We do not imply that one is " better " than the other; actually, some forms of psychic deprivation are more brutalizing than some uses of force. But it seems essential to us to analytically separate violence from other forms of victimization, if only so that its relationships to the other can be analyzed.

(or 62.03%) were reported to be peaceful, 7 (3.24%) as involving an act of obstruction, and 75 (34.72%) as violent.[8]

Of the 75 incidents which included violence, the reporting of 11 incidents was not sufficiently clear on this point to allow us to specify the initiator of the violence. The violence in 26 of them was initiated, according to the reports, not by the demonstrators themselves but by other groups—either those opposed to the demonstrators or their cause (in 17 incidents), or the police (in 9 cases). In 38 cases, the violence seems to have been started by the demonstrators—i.e., only in 17.5% of the total number of demonstrations.

6. *The public view of demonstrations*

Wide segments of the public do not distinguish between peaceful demonstrations, which are legal and constitutional means of political expressions, and violent demonstrations or riots. And these segments of the public condemn demonstrations indiscriminately. James Reston observed that "the prevailing mood of the country is against the demonstrators in the black ghettos and the universities," even though most of these demonstrations are peaceful.[9] "Certainly it is a matter of concern when Americans find the ordinary channels of discussion and decision so unresponsive that they feel forced to take their grievances to the street."[10] Rather than paying attention to the needs communicated by the demonstrations, the majority of the citizenry on the sidelines focuses its attention on the communicative acts themselves, and condemns both them and their participants. For instance, 74% of the adult public in a California poll expressed disapproval of the student demonstrations at Berkeley in 1964[11] although they were non-violent.

[8] See Appendix B for a list of all the demonstrations in our " sample ".
[9] *New York Times,* October 23, 1968.
[10] " Law and Order," *Life,* September 27, 1968.
[11] Colin Miller, " The Press and the Student Revolt," in Michael V. Miller and Susan Gilmore (eds.), *Revolution at Berkeley* (New York: Dial Press, 1965), p. 347.

A Harris Poll (September 27, 1965) reports that 68% of Americans find anti-Vietnam pickets "more harmful than helpful" (5%—more helpful than harmful). 68% versus 16% feel the same way about civil rights demonstrations, and the distribution of attitudes toward student demonstrations at colleges is very similar (65% versus 7%). A later poll shows that the public has grown even more critical of Negro "demonstration tactics"; those who disapprove of them have grown to 82%.[12]

Interpreting these findings poses one difficulty: they tap at one and the same time an attitude concerning a mode of political expression (demonstrations) and/or a substantive question (e.g., attitude toward the war). It should be noted, however, that the percent of the public disapproving of the war or favorable to civil rights is much higher than those tolerant of demonstrations in favor of these causes.

Second, the pollsters usually do not provide an opportunity for the respondents to separate peaceful from violent demonstrations. On the few occasions in which the public was explicitly asked about a specific peaceful event or about peaceful demonstrations, larger numbers approved of them than support demonstrations in general (including violent ones), but many still do not see the legitimacy of this mode of political expression. A sample of the general public was asked, " The leaders of the Poor People's March have emphasized that they are going to follow the non-violent ways of Martin Luther King Jr. Some people fear the march will lead to violence. Do you feel it is more right or more wrong for the Poor People's March to be held?" Only 26% of the people as a whole (and only 21% of the whites) felt that it was all right for the poor people to hold a march on Washington.[13]

Asked explicitly about the right to engage in *peaceful* demonstrations—" against the war in Vietnam "—40% of the people sampled in both December, 1966 and July, 1967, felt that the citizenry had no such right. 58% were prepared to

[12] Harris, June 5, 1967.
[13] Harris, June 10, 1968.

" accept " such demonstrations " as long as they are peaceful," leaving a major segment of the public unaware that such demonstrations have the same legal status as writing a letter to a Congressman or participating in a town meeting.

The situation is somewhat similar to the first appearances of organized, peaceful labor strikes. Not only the owners and managers of industrial plants but also broad segments of the public at the beginning of the century did not recognize the rights of workers to strike if their grievances were unheeded, and peacefully to picket factories if such actions did not involve violating the rights of others (e.g., occupying the plant or physically preventing people from coming or going). Strikes are much more widely accepted now (although some portions of the public still harbor some of the earlier reservations about them). " The majority (77% of those sampled) feel that the refusal to work is the ultimate and legitimate recourse for union members engaged in the process of collective bargaining."[14] " People find it perfectly understandable that workers will go out on strike for higher wages, better living standards, more fringe benefits and improved working conditions. They say that the strike is the only ultimate weapon of unions, is part of the free union system and in some cases is the only way to win demands " (Ibid.). There is not yet anything like such a general acceptance of the legitimacy of peaceful demonstrations, but such tolerance might develop just as it did for strikes.

It should be noted in this context that as more of the public learned to accept strikes, the occasions on which they erupted into violent confrontations became much less frequent. Of course, other factors are in part responsible for the decrease in labor-management violence, the most important of which seems to be the increased readiness to respond to the issues raised by the strikers rather than merely responding to the act of striking. Hopefully, reactions to peaceful demonstrations will undergo similar transformations both in the public mind and the relevant institutions.

[14] Harris, March 27, 1967.

7. The role of television

Demonstrations, or their equivalents, have occurred throughout history. In ancient days, protesting crowds at the market place or in front of the palace served to express mounting disaffection. In later days, parliaments frequently drew such attention.

> ". . . A public demonstration in favor of parliamentary reform was arranged for the 16th [of August, 1819] over which Hunt [a leading orator] would preside. In the interval the entire country was in a ferment of heated expectation. The mill hands engaged in mysterious drills, unarmed according to the radical organs, armed according to the Tory Press. And their intentions: To learn how to carry out without disorder the mass movements which would be involved when in their thousands, nay, in their tens of thousands, they assembled for a common demonstration. To prepare, replied the Tories, a violent revolution. Knots of workmen gathered in the streets of Manchester, hustled and insulted respectable citizens and their wives. The great day came. From all the towns of the neighborhood, unarmed and in perfect order, with flags flying and drums beating, squadrons of workers marched into Manchester."[15]

But the rise of demonstrations to the status of a prominent and daily instrument of political expression dates, we suggest, from the age of television. In this country, mass television was introduced in the early nineteen-fifties. In 1949, there were television sets in only 940,000 homes; by 1953, they were found in more than twenty million homes; by 1959, the number matched that of American families (45,500,000) and almost equalled the number of homes with radio sets. We hold though we cannot document this here, that the number of

---

[15] Elie Halevy, *The Liberal Awakening, 1815-1830* (New York: Barnes and Noble, 1961), pp. 64-65.

demonstrations in the pre-mass television decade (1948-1958) was much smaller than in the first television decade (1958-1968).

We do *not* suggest that television generated protest or mobilized black, poor, young, and growing numbers of other Americans to express their needs and demands more actively. Such mobilization is probably the result of many other factors, including the migration of Negroes from the South to the North, the return of Negroes with organizational experience from World War II, the increased numbers of college-educated citizens, and the War in Vietnam. (The spread of television, which brought images of enormous affluence to many homes in which the conditions were vastly different, may well qualify as another factor.)

What we do maintain is that television has played a key role in the evolution of this particular form of political expression and in the increasing frequency with which this form is applied, in effect, in creating demonstration democracy.

Demonstrations as a major political tool in this country began with the civil rights movement in the South.[16] The first acts of civil rights protest, the Montgomery Alabama bus boycott in 1956 and the lunch-counter sit-ins in 1960, were not widely televised, lending further support to our point that the *origin* of the protest is not the media. But once the media and protest linked up, during the marches in Albany, Georgia, 1962, and Birmingham, Alabama in 1963[17] (remember Bull Connor and his dogs), the efficacy of demonstrations as a mode of *expressing* protest became evident. This reached a television climax in such day-long events as the 1963 March on Washington and the 1965 March on Selma.

The role of television becomes clear when its special characteristics are taken into account. Television differs from other means of communication in that it adds pictures to

[16] Irving Howe, " The New ' Confrontation Politics ' is a Dangerous Game," *New York Magazine*, October 20, 1968, pages 28-ff.

[17] P. 11 and also p. 93 Anthony Lewis, *Portrait of a Decade* (New York : Random House, 1964), p. 11 and p. 93.

words, communicates instantly, *and* is national in its coverage. No other medium matches television on all these dimensions. Radio is only verbal. Newspapers are neither national nor instantaneous, and are long on words and short—by comparison—on pictures. The national weekly picture magazines come closer to television from this viewpoint, although they are, of course, far from immediate and much less frequent than television news. The pictures they carry in a week are flashed on the television screen in less than a minute to an audience which at least matches their readership in size.

It is doubtful that anyone involved in the early days of the civil rights movement was consciously seeking a new means of political expression especially suited to television, but those who organized the first marches could not help but note that they had found one. Moreover, they did not lose the older media in the process. Even today, a demonstration, despite its daily " routine " nature, gains more attention from the mass media (i.e., communicates more effectively) than any other legitimate political act by an equal number of citizens. As the needs of television and of the demonstrators are so intimately linked, demonstrations—of one kind or another—can be expected to continue as an integral part of the American political system so long as there is protest to express and television to communicate it. There may be some decrease in the news value of demonstrations as they become even more commonplace or as a result of deliberate network policy, but—we shall see—this is not necessarily desirable.

*   *   *

The rise in the number, frequency, scope, and " respectability " of demonstrations and their close link with television all suggest that demonstrations, as a major means through which protest can be expressed, are now and will remain part and parcel of the country's political processes and will not disappear when the war in Vietnam is over or the needs of the poor are met. For good or bad, they are now part of our

system. We turn, next, to a consideration of the effects of
demonstrations and ask how their positive consequences may
be enhanced while their dysfunctions may be curbed.

THE FUNCTIONS AND DYSFUNCTIONS OF DEMOCRATIC DEMONSTRATIONS

1. *An analytic orientation*

In part, a discussion of the advantages and disadvantages of
this particular form of political expression is an academic
exercise; even if it were decided that demonstrations are, in
balance, an undesirable political instrument, they cannot be
suppressed or otherwise eliminated any more than could television. Our purpose in the following analysis, therefore, is not
to provide a judgment on the relative value of demonstrations
but, rather, to gain a better sense of their dynamics and, above
all, the conditions under which they remain peaceful.

2. *A digression into political theory*

Before the relative merits and demerits of this political tool
can be directly assessed, a comment on the nature of political
instruments is necessary. Briefly, we see society as composed of
groups of citizens caught in a double bind: they share some
values and interests with all other citizens (as members of the
particular society), and they have some special needs of their
own. The needs of any one grouping may complement, com-
pete, or openly conflict with those of other member groups.
Politics is a process by which that which unites the member
groups is promoted and differences are reduced and " worked
out."

At each point in time, a viable society has both a pattern
of allocation which specifies the relative share of the national
assets each group can draw (which is never the same for all
groups) *and* mechanisms for working out reallocations (e.g.,

taxes and welfare services). Over time, a group of citizens may evolve new needs or a new awareness of old needs. In no society even in the most affluent one, can all the legitimate needs of all the citizens be met. In the short run, the inability of a society to respond to the needs of all of its members is even more pronounced. Hence, it is the task of the political process to convert new demands of social groups into political claims —for representation, appropriations and legislation—*and* to reduce these claims to a level which the system can handle without seriously alienating the members whose legitimate wants cannot be satisfied, at least " now."

This conversion process is affected by the extent to which the needs advanced by a group are legitimate in terms of the values subscribed to by the other groups (e.g., equality of opportunity) *and* the amount of social and political power the group is able to mobilize. Ideally, any increase in the social power of a group (e.g., due to an increase in its relative size) will be translated into a proportional increase in its political power (e.g., representation) *and* in the reallocation of the national assets as well as the redirection of national policy. Such a situation would constitute maximum responsiveness of the polity.

In fact, though, the national and local political centers are often slow in recognizing new needs or the aggravation of old ones and in reassessing the changing power of various social groups, especially those which are remote from these centers in terms of patterns of social behavior, modes of expression, etc. *There is, hence, frequently some degree of a double gap: of communication and of power.* That is, the political centers would be more accommodating were they able to " read " the changing social scene more accurately; and were social power more readily convertible into political power, the centers would be forced more quickly to restructure their policies or themselves so that they would become more in accord with their changing constituencies. These statements do not assume that the local and national centres are anxious to initiate reforms, especially major ones and ones which erode the privileges of social groups particularly close to these centres. But improved communication would allow the centres to *anticipate* changes which will have to be made later in any case and the opportunity to introduce them earlier before tensions increase and violence occurs. Whether they would initiate change or not is another question; but such behavior would be justified in terms of the centres' self-interest if for no other reason.

When the upward channels of communication are not effective, power relations among groups in the society and the distribution of political power will tend to grow further apart. The greater the discrepancies between the social and the political patterns of a nation, the greater the internal tensions, conflicts, and potential for violence. Societies which are *very severely* disjointed in this way gain little from seeking to improve communication and improve " conversion " of social into political power; such improvements will only delay the necessary and inevitable fundamental readjustment of the political structure. On the other hand, improvement of the means of communication and power conversion is an effective way to reform societies which have not reached the level of such extreme dissociation of the social from the political. The United States, despite indications considered by some as pointing in the opposite direction, is, in our judgment, for reasons spelled out elsewhere,[18] well within the range of societies which may be reformed, although the process needs to be greatly accelerated and expanded in scope. This assumption underlies the following examination.

3. *Comparison of political means: Some functions of demonstrations*

On August 26, 1968, Secretary of Health, Education and Welfare, Wilbur J. Cohen, facing a discourteous but peaceful demonstration at the American Sociological Association meeting in Boston, told the young sociologists who were demon-

[18] Amitai Etzioni, *The Active Society* (New York : The Free Press, 1968), especially chapters 15 to 18.

strating that if they wished a change, they should fight for it through the ballot box. Many Americans, probably the majority, share the view that voting is the avenue for the communication of needs and conversion of social demands and power into political power and action. The textbook model of democracy sees shifts in votes as the mechanism for keeping society and the state closely related. Actually, this is not how it works out, for several reasons which are quite well known. For one, the American system of representation still favors residents of rural, conservative areas; it under-represents urban centers, minorities, and the poor. In the four years between presidential elections other modes of political expression are needed, as the president is free, we have learned, to favor one policy while campaigning but to follow another after the election. That he may not be reelected is small comfort; nor is there any guarantee that future presidents will heed the electorate's voice. In 15 elections out of 37, since 1824, the President has been elected by less than 50% of the nation's voters. (In three elections, the loser got more votes than the winner.) Even when they are in a minority, the needs of those whose candidate lost must also be heeded. Above all, most legislation and major administrative acts are supported or " cleared " by the major relevant interest groups—e.g., the lobbies of labor unions, manufacturing associations, the gun owners, the farmers—and *not* via the election process. Hence, unorganized groups and citizens at large have at best a disproportionately small and after-the-fact effect, and at worst do not even know that legislation or a change of administration policy has taken place.

Demonstrations provide an interim election tool, especially for those groups which have no special representation (or lobbies) and for the public at large. Demonstrations may serve to countervail specific pressure groups (e.g., the wine growers in California) among those whose needs are the most neglected and who cannot use other political means nearly as effectively as the more affluent, educated, and politically experienced groups. Letter writing, petitions, advertisements in newspapers, campaign contributions, and lobbying—and almost all political tools other than demonstrations—are particularly suited to the privileged rather than to the under-privileged groups. To use them effectively requires money, education, and organizational experience.

Even voting is less accessible to those citizens who demonstrate most—poor, Negroes, and youth. In the 1964 presidential election only 53% of those with an income of less than $3,000 voted as compared with the 62% overall turnout, and with 85% of those earning $10,000 or more. Only 51% of the 10 million persons under 25 voted in 1964 compared to 70% of the older people. 88% of the college graduates voted as compared with 51% of those with eight years of schooling or less. The low voting rates are often not due to the group itself: e.g., youth are more mobile and hence cannot meet their residence requirements; the poor are under more pressure from employers than are the non-poor not to vote, etc. It should also be noted that many of the demonstrators are in the 18-21 age category. They are not eligible to vote in the national elections despite their demand for such a right and wide support from responsible leaders across the nation. Eighteen-year-olds are quite mature and politically concerned nowadays; they are, it has often been pointed out, old enough to be asked to die for their country. Thus their taking to the streets is further encouraged by keeping closed to them the doors of the voting places.

Economists refer to a " comparative advantage " a country may have in the production of certain kinds of products which " compensate " for its disadvantage in other areas; this concept may be applied to political tools and productivity. Each social group may be said to find a comparative advantage in one political tool or another; those disadvantaged in the use of more conventional techniques find in demonstrations a tool that operates to their relative advantage. Thus they compensate, to a degree, for their deficiencies elsewhere.

While demonstrations are becoming more acceptable and respectable, they still carry a considerable amount of social stigma which explains why they are less "natural" means of expression for the middle and upper classes. The lower classes, minorities, and youth—who either have different norms in regard to such matters as neatness, walking on the street, and public display, or who "don't mind" violating rules of etiquette—can employ this tool (and have done so frequently). *Thus, in sum, demonstrations help to reduce the inequality among the member groupings of society in terms of their access to political tools; they add to the tools particularly appropriate to the middle and upper classes, one which is especially suited to the under-privileged and young.*

4. The dysfunctions of demonstrations

As political tools, demonstrations do have several dysfunctions; some are quite limited while others are much more serious. Relatively easy to handle are their tendencies to "flatten" the message and to misrepresent; much more troublesome is the relatively high probability that peaceful demonstrations will escalate into violent ones. These dysfunctions and the ways in which they may be overcome are reviewed one at a time. First, though, a methodological consideration which is pertinent to the following discussion should be stressed; *none* of the available tools is without flaws. Voters have been bribed and deliberately misinformed. Ballot boxes have been stuffed. Writing letters to the President and members of Congress has been organized by lobbies, etc. It is, hence, not useful to compare any one political tool to an abstract ideal; each must be compared to the other. And the place of each in the total array of political instruments must be taken into account, as some help to close gaps left by the others.

4.1 The "flattening" effect

Most political tools suffer from the fact that as upward means of communication they transmit only messages which are limited in scope and superficial (or "flat") in content. A voter has one vote per candidate or party once every two, four, or six years with which to communicate his approval or disapproval on scores of issues. (In national presidential elections, each citizen ought to have *at least two votes* which he could split, one for domestic and one for foreign affairs.) By comparison, petitions and letters are *much* richer in content and allow the expression of more subtle gradations, the importance of which will become evident below.

Demonstrations have a flattening effect on the political process, especially if they replace rather than supplement other modes of political expression for a specific group. The slogans and signs carried tend to reduce positions to highly simplified statements often obscuring more subtle differences and expositions. The fact that the placard or banner seems to have substituted to a considerable extent for the pamphlet is one reason that contemporary protest is frequently so Know-Nothing in nature; there is little outlet and encouragement for intellectual activity. Demonstrations put a premium on gestures, " props ", and vividness—all emotive devices—to the detriment of verbal exposition, the basis of intellectually rich and subtle communication. Thus, demonstrators who wear bizarre clothing (or none at all), who carry offensive objects, and so on, attract much more attention than those who attempt to speak reasonably and with dignity about their group's needs. Demagogic speakers receive more publicity than " cooler " spokesmen. Obstructionist tactics gain more attention than peaceful ones, and acts of violence—the most of all. But both obstructionist and violent acts have a " flattening " effect. In contrast, participation in a town meeting, debate, the writing of a pamphlet, or even door-to-door campaigning requires the citizen to sort out his thoughts, express himself in a way others can understand and take their position into account. To block a passage or set a fire requires none of these attributes. It gains a lot of attention but communicates very little.

A recent significant development in the mass media serves to correct, to some degree, the " flattening " effect of demonstrations as a political tool, a correction which could be further extended. The media's coverage of demonstrations used to focus primarily on the "colorful" aspects such as the demonstrators' appearance, slogans, or clashes with counter-demonstrators or the police. Recently, however, the media seem to rely more and more upon *interviews* with both the leaders of the demonstrations and representatives of the groups or institutions against which they demonstrate. Such interviews greatly enrich the communicative content of the action and put greater value on level-headed, articulate leaders and peaceful demonstrations.

In several instances the media have called the attention of the viewers to the fact that they were being deliberately aroused by clever demonstrators. For example, the media reported that television, radio and press representatives were invited ahead of time to be at a specific intersection at a given hour to see a "spontaneous" outbreak of protest, or informed the viewers that demonstrations had been re-scheduled to take place at prime television time, or so as not to conflict with another newsworthy event. Such reporting reduces the effect of manipulation of the viewers and indirectly increases the benefit of substantive expositions.

The obvious recommendation is that some representatives of the mass media, especially the television networks, should themselves form a committee to formulate guide lines for accurate, subtle, ethical reporting. It is unlikely that the existing defects in the reporting of demonstrations, which often result in flattening communication, can be completely overcome; in part, they are inherent in the nature of the media and the demonstrations. It seems, though, that they can be mitigated considerably.

4.2 *"Unrepresentative" representatives and "false" demonstrations*

Representative structures as a rule do not mirror their constituencies with any degree of accuracy. Professor R. Dahl, of Yale, in a study of American voting patterns, computed an index of advantage in which the index would be 1 if actual and proportional representations were equal. His figures, based on votes cast in the 1952 election, show a score of 14.8 for Nevada as compared to 0.17 for New York.[19] At that time, a majority of the votes in the United States Senate could be cast by Senators representing less than 15 per cent of the American voters. Underrepresented societal groupings included not only Negroes but also sharecroppers, migrant workers, wage earners, and coal miners.

The median age of present-day Americans in 1967 was reported as twenty-eight, but among the House and Senate chairmen it was 67. Nor did congressional leadership reflect modern America in terms of religion. In 1967, seventeen of the twenty committee chairmen in the House were white, Anglo-Saxon Protestants. In the Senate, Allen Ellender from Catholic Louisiana was the only non-WASP chairing a committee. Geographically, the former Confederate States of America, with one-fifth of the United States population, provided nine out of sixteen chairmen in the Senate and eleven out of twenty in the House.[20] Professor S. Stouffer found that the leadership of 14 voluntary associations he surveyed was about 30% more liberal than their memberships.[21] The overwhelming majority of the public favors stricter gun control legislation. A Louis Harris Survey in the *Washington Post* on April 22, 1968 reported that " a cross section of 1634 homes was asked . . . ' Do you favor or oppose Federal laws which would control the sales of guns, such as making all persons register all gun purchases no matter where they buy them?' " The results were : 71% favor; 23% oppose; 6% not sure. But the majority of Congressmen did not support such measures.

[19] Robert A. Dahl, *A Preface to Democratic Theory* (Chicago : University of Chicago Press, 1956) pp. 114-ff.

[20] News release from Joseph S. Clark, U.S. Senator from Pennsylvania, March 31, 1967. p. 3.

[21] Samuel A. Stouffer, *Communism v. Conformity and Civil Liberties* (Garden City, New York : Doubleday, 1955), p. 29 ff.

A relatively close approximation between representatives and their constituencies is the best that can realistically be expected. Indeed, major political theorists have argued that some latitude is essential if the representatives are to carry out their missions.

Demonstrators are often similarly more dedicated and " extreme " than most of the members of the groups for whom they claim to speak. This " bias " can be overcome by responding to the needs of the group itself rather than to those expressed by its self appointed spokesmen. Labor became a peaceful member grouping in democratic societies—in Britain, Scandinavia, West Germany, as well as other nations —without these societies being forced to accept the notions advanced in the Marxist argot of many of the earlier labor leaders; for example, to satisfy demands for nationalization of the means of production. Similarly, not every demand of the black militants must be taken at face value or viewed as expressing the basis on which Negro-Americans will become full members of the American society and polity. Nor do occasional Vietcong flags and cliché-ridden speeches about United States imperialism indicate that most of the anti-war demonstrators identify with the Communist cause.

In addition to those expressing a concern with the " extremism " of the demonstrators, we find those who hold that demonstrations are fomented by " outsider agitators," by persons whose positions are very different from those of the group they mobilize; e.g., Southern whites frequently allege that Negroes in the South do not actually desire the goals advocated by the civil rights movement but that these are imported by leftist or Northern " agitators."

As with many a stereotype, this view does contain an element of truth. The mobilizers are often atypical; but this can be the case with all other modes of political expression as well, for example, the white political machine in black districts of Chicago in earlier days, or the students which campaigned for Eugene McCarthy. *But* in the long run such outsiders cannot mobilize large numbers of group members, *especially* for demonstrations, unless they appeal to a genuine need of the members and no other effective forms of political mobilization are operative. We say this holds particularly for demonstrations because participation in them requires more time, energy, and exposure to opposition than do other modes of political expression. A person will, under social pressure, sign his name to a petition with which he does not agree more readily than he will demonstrate for a cause in which he does not believe, under similar circumstances. It would seem much easier to bribe a poor person to change his vote (formerly done with coal or whiskey) than to get him out to demonstrate.[22] And while a demagogue can elicit strong emotions in some demonstrations, we expect that in most cases he can do so only where a political vacuum exists and where frustrated desires have found no other outlet.

The size of a demonstration is, thus, a fair—although far from accurate and often a somewhat conservative—indicator of the " size " of the group's unmet need and social power. 250,000 whites and Negroes did not come to march on Washington D.C., in August, 1963 because of a group of agitators. And most of the 200,000 New Yorkers who marched in the April 1967 mobilization against the war in Vietnam were there because they objected to the war. It is true that *additional* motives may exist: some young people meet dates on marches, and other are exhibitionistic. But again, this holds for all political activities and activists. For example, studies show that one reason citizens are active in political clubs is that they meet their friends there.[23]

When there is no " real " cause, or the mobilizers repeatedly over-state their case, they are often left to demonstrate alone. To illustrate: In October 1968, Columbia University's new acting president, Andrew Cordier, introduced several limited

[22] D. W. Brogan, *Politics in America* (Garden City, N.Y.: Doubleday, 1960), pp. 85-95.

[23] Samuel J. Eldersveld, *Political Parties* (Chicago: Rand McNally, 1964), pp. 295-303. See also S. Brown, " Fun can be politics," *The Reporter,* Vol. 21 (November 12, 1959), pp. 27-28.

reforms. Soon after, attempts at mobilization of the student body by the same radical groups which had, the previous spring, marshaled thousands of students against the authoritarian and unresponsive regime of the former president, met with almost no success. Several demonstrations were scheduled but drew less than 200 students. In frustration, S.D.S. tried to find new causes and create new incidents. But the University blocked the group's attempt to interrupt fall registration by mobilizing its own guards who applied minimum force, thus preventing the inciting effects of the police brutality of April 1968. When the group later broke into a building to hold an assembly, which violated one of the University's rules, Cordier was reported ready to suspend the S.D.S. charter. Mass support for S.D.S. swelled up again but disappeared when Cordier announced that he would take no such action. Finally, the frustrated S.D.S. conceded defeat, reorganized itself, and turned to " educational " and " mobilization " efforts to broaden its base of support. It is not suggested that peace will now prevail forever on the Columbia campus; the reforms which have been initiated are only a very small fraction of those needed. If the tranquility that exists as these lines are written is not used as a breathing spell in which to introduce wider reforms and to mobilize the moderate students and faculty on the side of the reforming University, the campus will soon be ready for new incidents and mass mobilization. Thus, the developments of October 1968 illustrate that agitation succeeds—as the radicals keep reminding each other— only when the situation is " ripe," when there are both legitimate needs which have not been met and a dearth of institutionalized means of political expression. Such " ripeness ", in turn, cannot be generated by a group of demagogues, however skillful and resourceful they be.

While it took longer, the change of administration at Berkeley, from the authoritarian Chancellor Strong to liberal Hynes, had a similar effect on the potency of radicalist action. In other situations, such as in the ghettos, where more basic needs have longer been neglected, and hopes often crushed, it will take far more than a change of municipal administration and the initiation of reforms to restore peace. But we still expect the same basic "law" will apply. When people have institutionalized channels to express themselves and channels which are effective, why should they take to the streets?

4.3 *Volatility*

We saw that on several accounts demonstrations are rather like other political tools; there is, though, one danger which is uniquely theirs: a tendency to escalate from peaceful to obstructionist and from obstructionist to violent action, both in the course of a single demonstration and, over time, in terms of the kind of action initiated to advance a given cause. We have already noted that the overwhelming majority of demonstrations are peaceful; the violent sub-set, though, must not be ignored. In the following pages we first raise the question of the conditions under which violent demonstrations occur. We then turn to the problem of the political consequences of actions designed to increase the probabilities that they will remain peaceful.

a. *Excessive restrictions*: First in terms of sequence, if not of frequency, is the extent to which undue restrictions are placed on peaceful demonstrations. Demonstrations must be limited to some degree in terms of time, place, and format. For example, no community can be expected to allow a small number of demonstrators to block a major traffic artery during rush hours. Thus, there is some regulation of peaceful demonstrations in most communities.

Consistent with the reluctance of a large part of the public to recognize the legitimacy of peaceful demonstrations, we find that the authorities are apt to abuse their quite necessary power to regulate demonstrations—in an attempt to suppress them. While occasionally such excessive restrictions prevent demonstrations from taking place, in most instances they appear to lead to an increase in the size of demonstrations because persons who are concerned with the general issue of freedom of political expression may join with the originally aggrieved groups. Such restrictions also increase the probabilities that a demonstration will turn violent either because the demonstration is defined as illegal by the authorities and the police are called in; or because the constitutionality of the restrictions is being tested by the demonstrators; or because it proves impracticable to keep the demonstration within the unreasonable limits set for it.

We have not conducted a study of the limitations imposed by the Chicago police on anti-war demonstrations during the August 1968 Democratic convention, but they seem to be a case in point.[24] On February 2, 1965, Dr. King and 263 others were arrested in Selma, Alabama, for parading without a permit—which they could not obtain. A demonstration at the draft center in Oakland, California on December 19, 1967, became much larger when it became known that Oakland would not allow it to take place. The April 1968 crisis at Columbia University was triggered by a typical ban on *peaceful* demonstrations. The students prior to this time had sought permission to demonstrate indoors at a place where, and a time when, they would not disturb the work of the University. A committee was appointed by the president of the University to study the issue (possibly a quite unnecessary delay in permitting the students to exercise a basic right). The Committee recommended that indoor demonstrations be allowed.

"On September 25, 1967, there issued from President Kirk's office a statement of policy that included the rule: 'picketing or indoor demonstrations may not be conducted within any University building.' No explanation

[24] Russell Baker lost his sense of humor when he saw that ". . .young people try to sleep on the grass and, for this impertinence, get their skulls cracked and their ribs knocked by the gentlemen whom Mayor Daley calls ' the finest police force in the country.' Using the public grass after midnight can be a dangerous provocation to a policeman." (*New York Times*, August 28, 1968.)

accompanied the announcement. The committee which had worked long and hard in developing a less restrictive rule was in no way consulted . . . A rule of great concern to students had been issued without participation by the faculty or themselves."[25]

When the students did demonstrate before the April 1968 crisis, six were expelled, triggering a sit-in on their behalf which led to a violent confrontation. After this confrontation, the University accepted new rules allowing indoor demonstrations.

It is not suggested that this was *the* issue which created the April 1968 crisis; the right to demonstrate is usually a secondary issue. But it *is* an issue which gives radicals the support of many moderates, swells the ranks of the demonstrators, and, above all, is a major factor in producing a violent confrontation where otherwise a peaceful demonstration might have taken place.

We strongly recommend, as part of our general argument for increasing acceptance of peaceful demonstrations, that provisions be made for them which are as broad and flexible as possible.[26] Attempts to constrict them in the name of public safety are often a major violation of the constitutional rights of the demonstrators and a means of endangering the public through greatly increasing the probability that the demonstration will be violent.

b. *Provocation by " by-standers "*: In recent years, most violent confrontations have occurred between demonstrators and the police. However, in earlier periods, inter-group clashes were much more common. Conflicts between Catholics and

---

[25] *The Cox Commission Report: Crisis at Columbia* (New York: Vintage Books, 1968), p. 50.

[26] Two 1968 Supreme Court rulings seem valuable from this viewpoint. One upheld the right of persons protesting the war in Vietnam to set up facilities to distribute their pamphlets and leaflets in public places, such as railroad stations and bus terminals. The other defined as unconstitutional denials of the right to hold a rally, even for public safety reasons, unless those who sought to assemble a protest were first heard.

Protestants led to the Andros Insurrection in Massachusetts in 1689. Irishmen and Negroes clashed in the draft riots of 1863.[27] Anti-Chinese riots occurred in Los Angeles and San Francisco in the 1870's, and anti-Negro riots in 1919 and 1920. We fear the return to such clashes in the near future. Some recent triggering of violence by attacks on the demonstrators by other citizens with differing views has already taken place. At Columbia University in April, 1967, there was a fist fight initiated by the athletes against S.D.S. demonstrators who were protesting recruiting on the campus by the Marine Corps. Eggs, paint, and tomatoes were thrown at anti-war demonstators by counter-demonstrators in New York City on October 15, 1965. Hell's Angels attacked marchers at Berkeley on this same date. In Milwaukee, Wisconsin, a peaceful demonstration, led by Rev. James E. Groppi in the first week of September 1967, ended in violence when Polish-American onlookers from the city's South Side showered Negro marchers with bottles and stones. In some Chicago suburbs, during non-violent marches led in August 1966 by Martin Luther King, Jr., Negroes were attacked by whites. In these and many other cases, peaceful demonstrations were turned into violent incidents by others than the demonstrators.

It might be said, and it has been said, that the demonstrators provoke these incidents: leftist students provoked fist fights at Columbia University by crowding a hall in which there was a Marine recruiter, or Negroes marching in Polish-American neighborhoods to demand open housing provoked the residents. But this is to disregard the constitutionality, legality, moral legitimacy, and sociological efficacy of peaceful demonstrations. Obviously, to avoid the violence which resulted both from attacks on the demonstrators *and* from the blockage of this avenue of political expression, it is necessary that full police protection be extended to the demonstrators and that the political leadership clearly and repeatedly em-

[27] James McCague, *The Second Rebellion* (New York: Dial Press, 1968).

phasize the legitimacy of peaceful demonstrations. The leaders should, in effect, use such occasions to educate the public to the acceptance of this form of political action.

c. *The police as a trigger*: It is obvious to some and shocking to others that the police—the agency charged with protecting the peace—is one force which turns peaceful demonstrations into violent ones. This is hardly a new phenomenon. Halevy describes a 19th century incident as follows:

" Sixty thousand men and women had gathered in St. Peter's Fields when a carriage arrived containing Henry Hunt and his assistants, overpowered with delight at a spectacle more imposing than any they had yet witnessed. Scarcely had Hunt obtained silence and begun to speak when a platoon of cavalry was seen forcing its way through the crowd towards the platform. Surrounded and threatened by the masses who stood blocking their way, the cavalrymen drew their swords and struck out to right and left. A company of hussars hastened to their assistance. The crowd took to their heels, knocking one another down in their panic. Within ten minutes the place had been cleared. The banners which decked the platform were thrown into the gutter, and the demonstrators chased through the streets at the point of the sword. Eleven persons were killed, including two women, and several hundred wounded."[28]

A demonstration whose peaceful beginnings were reported earlier ended in this way:

". . . six million signatures were claimed (though there may have been only half that number) and a great demonstration was called on Kennington Common in

[28] Elie Halevy, *The Liberal Awakening, 1815-1830* (New York: Barnes and Noble, 1961), pp. 64-65.

London to give the petition a send-off. The demonstrators were peaceable enough; but the government, fearing French agents and Irish rebels even more than English rioters, mustered 170,000 special constables and a large military force under the aged Duke of Wellington to disperse them. It was, wrote Lord Palmerston, ' a glorious day, the Waterloo of peace and order.' It was also to all intents and purposes, the end of Chartism as a national political movement."[29]

Actually, in the month and areas we studied, we found nine incidents in which the violence was initiated by the police, about one every three days. In some cases, the incendiary role of the police was an indirect one and/or within that grey area between legality and extra-legality. In others, the police outrightly initiated and, in effect, monopolized the violent acts without any discernible legal foundation—what one observer called " a riot by men in blue uniforms."[30]

Violence is repeatedly generated by the use of excessive force on the part of the police, in incidents much like those reported by the Kerner Commission. "Almost invariably the incident that ignites disorder arises from police action."[31] Basically this same pattern was found in Cleveland in July 1968.[32]

In an incident in Washington, during the period we studied, a white policeman, David Roberts, killed 23-year-old Elijah Bennett (black) following an attempt to detain him for jaywalking. It was alleged that the two were struggling. The coroner's jury, " apparently convinced that Pvt. David Roberts

[29] George Rude, *The Crowd in History, 1730-1846* (New York: John Wiley & Sons, 1964), pp. 181-182.

[30] Professor Gary Marx of Harvard at the meetings of the American Political Science Association in Washington D.C., September 5, 1968.

[31] *The Report of the National Advisory Commission on Civil Disorders* (New York: Bantam Books, 1968), p. 206.

[32] For a careful account following weeks of investigation by a team of reporters, see the *New York Times*, September 2, 1968.

fired more in rage than in self-defense," returned a verdict of willful homicide,[33] although a Federal grand jury ruled later that there were no grounds for criminal prosecution. In the three days following this incident, there were several incidents in the streets of the area in which Bennett had been shot, including teenagers who blocked traffic and broke a number of store windows.[34] It is this latter kind of conduct which the groups who oppose demonstrations point, although its relation to action by the police is direct and obvious.

These incidents, though, involved riots, which are largely or wholly spontaneous, and police action is often the act of an individual. When police action turns a demonstration into a violent incident, this action is usually premeditated and involves large numbers of policemen, acting in the presence of their commanding officers.

A second category of such incidents is those in which the police clearly used excessive force either to impose legal limitations (which include such " grey " legalities as many Southern regulations), to deal with obstructions, or to establish unreasonable limitations on peaceful demonstrations. At Columbia University in April 1968, many policemen, according to well-documented accounts, used excessive force. In effect, they assaulted students who were not resisting them or were just observing the police action—turning an obstructionist into a violent incident. The Chicago police had a similar effect on a peaceful demonstration in the park during the 1968 Democratic Convention.

Finally, there are some incidents in which the police acted violently in situations that had no possible connection with law enforcement. The details surrounding the murder of Negroes in the Algiers Motel[35] may never be fully revealed, although the outlines seem fairly clear. The attack by 150 off-

---

[33] William Raspberry, " Facts in Killing by Policemen Need Thorough Airing," *The Washington Post,* October 20, 1968.
[34] *The Washington Post,* October 16, 1968.
[35] In Detroit in August, 1967.

duty, out-of-uniform policemen and some others on a group of Black Panthers and white sympathizers on the sixth floor of the Brooklyn Criminal Court Building on October 19, 1968 is completely unambiguous. The policemen did not deny their role but argued, in their defense, that "the assault was a spontaneous thing, not anticipated by the organizers."[36] This incident differs from others primarily in the superficiality of the injuries the victims sustained and in the clarity of the documentation (press reporters were present).[37] We, thus, agree with Adam Yarmolinsky, Professor of law at Harvard, who stated, "it is plain enough now that rioting by big city police is a clear and present danger to domestic tranquility in the United States."[38]

It has been suggested that some incidents in which the police used excessive force were "provoked" by the demonstrators' "foul" language, their hurling insults at the police, or their untidy appearance ("the police speak for the community"). Needless to say, a professional police force should not be able to be provoked by such conduct. If the demonstrators are behaving illegally, they may be prosecuted or even arrested, but assaulting them is, in itself, clearly against the law. If law enforcement authorities openly flaunt the law—and go unpunished when they do so—how can the demonstrators be expected to keep the peace? Especially dangerous is

[36] David Burnham, "Police Say Attack Was Spontaneous," *New York Times,* October 20, 1968.

[37] Another incident is reported in the following terms:
"Off-duty police officers have been accused of attacking and beating Negro youths, the sons of prominent citizens. City officials are convinced the accusations are correct, and Mayor Jerome P. Cavanagh has complained that a 'blue curtain' of silence among the police has hampered the investigation." Jerry M. Flint, "Negroes Accuse Police in Detroit," *New York Times,* November 10, 1968.
Most of the 43 persons who died in Detroit were killed by police and National Guard bullets—not by the rioters.
Typical newspaper report reads: "9 police cleared in 3 Negro Deaths; U.S. Jury in South Carolina Refuses to Indict them." *New York Times,* November 9, 1968.

[38] "Rioting by Police Becomes a Problem," *Washington Post,* September 14, 1968.

the conception that some police units seem to subscribe to, that beating up persons they view as offenders substitutes for the need to arrest and charge them. Thus, most Columbia students who were beaten were not arrested, and those arrested were not beaten. Other units use arrest as a punishment and not as a measure to hold the person until he is charged.

Aside from the obvious injustice, such police conduct turns peaceful demonstrations into violent ones. We shall continue to argue below that peaceful demonstrations are a very useful instrument in our society, and that they should be separated as much as possible from violent ones in the public's (and authorities') minds. Police riots have the opposite effect. They help to blur the line between the two kinds of demonstrations, when, in fact, it needs to be sharpened; they tend to block an essential channel of political expression; and tend to increase the possibility of violence in future demonstrations. The way the police can be made more professional in general and more respectful of citizens' right to demonstrate in particular is a subject beyond our domain here, but we strongly recommend all possible measures be taken to professionalize police handling of demonstrations, i.e., to train them to restrain themselves in the enforcement of the law within legal bounds in face of mounting provocations. The London police showed the way when it refused to lose its " cool " when deliberately provoked by a Maoist faction of a large anti-war demonstration in October 1968. It won the praise of the government, press, and public, and allowed the demonstration to close as it began—peacefully.

d. *Provocation by demonstrators*: The proportion of demonstrations in which violence is initiated by the demonstrators is not high: 38 out of 216 in the period we studied. The National Student Association study, which combines violent with obstructionist acts, reports that 41 of the demonstrations studied involved some such action but usually not a violent one. While this cannot be documented here, it is our impression that during the Johnson Administration, demonstrations grew more obstructionist and more violent, as frustration in the cities and on the campuses rose, and confidence in the political system declined.[39]

In the majority of those incidents in which violence was initiated by the demonstrators, the violence seems not to have been premeditated. The following is an example:

FIRE IN BUFFALO IS LAID TO YOUTHS RAMPAGING
AFTER POLITICAL RALLY.

BUFFALO, Oct. 18—What started out as a peaceful rally for Dick Gregory, the Presidential candidate, erupted into 12 hours of vandalism in the predominantly Negro East Side last night and early today.

At least 13 persons were arrested as roving gangs of teen-agers smashed windows and kept firefighters on the run, turning in 66 false alarms and then pelting the engines and firemen with rocks and bottles.

The rally supported Mr. Gregory and protested an alleged lack of police action in the murder of a 17-year-old Negro after the appearance of George C. Wallace here October 4.

The youth was struck in the back by a shot fired from a passing car and the police have been unable to locate the unknown assailant.[40]

In a few cases, the violence seems more likely to have been planned. For instance, following several days of unrest at New York University, over the dismissal of John F. Hatchett from his post as director of the University's Afro-American Student Center, " two small bombs were exploded, fire hoses and telephone wires cut, locks damaged and toilets plugged."[41] Typically in these cases, the violence is small in scale and against property rather than persons.

Contrary to the testimony given before the Commission on the Causes and Prevention of Violence by J. Edgar Hoover and in line with testimony of Attorney General Ramsey Clark, it is our finding and firsthand observation that on very

[39] Amitai Etzioni, " America's Alienated Majority," *The New Leader,* November 4, 1968.
[40] *New York Times,* October 19, 1968.
[41] Charles Grutzner, " Vandalism at N.Y.C. in Hatchett Protest," *New York Times,* October 15, 1968.

few occasions in the post-war United States are most of those involved in a sizeable demonstration, extremists who seek a violent confrontation. Nor are such violent extremists apt to be the leaders of demonstrations. Frequently, though, there are *some* extremists among the demonstrators and even among the leaders. Often the peaceful demonstrators seek to control their violent colleagues.

A recommendation addressed to those who seek to enhance peaceful demonstrations follows from this discussion. This is somewhat unorthodox and hence should be explained. The author of this document is particularly interested in policy research, i.e., in research which leads to the formulation and reformulation of public policy. Such research has inevitably a normative direction; it is not neutral and will not serve equally well a Stalinist totalitarian and a truly democratic government. In the case at hand, the commitment is to the activation of society, the reduction of alienation, the fundamental transformation of society so that it becomes authentically responsive to the needs of all its members without alienating non-members.

Such a position cannot be maintained if the policy researchers address themselves only to those in power—to the government or to presidential commissions. The preceding pages speak, in effect, first of all to local authorities (about the professionalization of the police) and to the conservative segments of the public (about their need to understand the legality and legitimacy of peaceful demonstrations). Now, peaceful demonstrators are to be subjected to some unsought, unsolicited advice.

For those who seek to demonstrate peacefully, it seems advisable to exclude, from the outset, demonstrators who subscribe to a philosophy of violence or seek to use violent tactics. Such action is recommended because, apart from the question of whether normative conditions under which violence may be condoned now prevail, many groups which seek to demonstrate *peacefully* become involved in violent incidents because a small *minority* of their members (or co-demonstrators) push them unwillingly in this direction. If the majority of the demonstrators were in favor of violence, the issue would be quite different, but the argument that violent demonstrators must be tolerated rather than expelled for the sake of solidarity is a naïve one. The differences among those who demonstrate are widely known to the press and public in any case. Further, the notion that violent demonstrators can be kept under control often turns out to be false. Above all, such tactical matters should not be allowed to cloud the major issue: peaceful demonstrations are an integral part of democratic politics, violent ones are not.

Non-violent civil disobedience is to be accepted only under certain very special circumstances when due process has been exhausted, when democracy is only operative "on paper," and when the laws which are challenged are themselves undemocratic. The nature and the proper forms of political expression are debatable issues which merit much more consideration; it is, however, essential that these issues not be settled by fiat. A violent minority should not be allowed to impose its views and tactics on a majority which clearly does not consider violence legitimate, either in any case or in a particular situation. Such an imposition of views can be avoided by stressing the differences between peaceful and violent demonstrations and by avoiding obstructionist behavior which tends to blur the line between them, making it more likely that a non-violent demonstration will turn into a violent confrontation.

Since demonstrators wishing a violent confrontation do not always identify themselves, and "security screening" is both distasteful and ineffective, peaceful demonstrators have taken such steps as the following to ensure that a particular demonstration will remain peaceful:

i) made explicit public statements before a demonstration stressing that non-violence is essential to the action contemplated;

ii) requested commitments to this effect from all leaders and groups of demonstrators (and, in effect, from every individual demonstrator);

iii) organized a large number of demonstrators into small groups with leaders who know the members and were responsible for their conduct; and

iv) provided marshals to deal with incendiary situations if and as they arose, and before they spread.

Perhaps the clearest example of the effectiveness of the above measures is the March on Washington in August 1963. Dire predictions of violence proved completely unfounded and major civil rights legislation was soon passed.

e. *The role of the media*: Much has been made of the very few documented incidents in which the media has " egged on " demonstrators to " act up " in order to gain more attention. Much more often the demonstrators " anticipate " the media and divine its character; it is a commonplace observation among demonstrators that acts of obstruction (and, even more so, of violence) gain the attention of the media and thus the " ear of the country."

Unfortunately the demonstrators, in their urge to communicate, seem to have confused the size of exposure (square inches in the papers, footage on television), with persuasion of the viewers. We would like to stress first that the *less* dissonant the mode and substance of a communication is, the less exposure it *may gain but the more effect it will have.* Pray-ins achieved more for the civil rights movement than vandalism, and peaceful marches—even heckling at political rallies—more than draft card burning for stopping the war.[42] Those inclined to obstructionist or violent demonstrations may argue that peaceful demonstrations did not gain justice or peace and hence they " must " turn to more extreme means. But these did not transform America overnight either. There

---

[42] These statements are based on implications of research conducted by Leon Festinger and other students of dissonance as well as on public opinion polls.

is only so much that can be achieved by *any* tool of political expression; the question is not which will deliver any and all goals, but of their relative efficacy. In contemporary America, peaceful demonstrations seem to be more effective in terms of mobilizing *wide* support than any other form of demonstration. Nor does the search for exposure in the media point only to violence. Violent acts gain extra exposure because they shock; basic norms of the community are violated. But as the demonstrators discovered, other acts *which entail no violence*, are similarly effective. Those include disrobing in public, carrying an enemy flag, etc. (They often entail some measure of civil disobedience.) Peaceful demonstrations are, in our judgment, the most effective communicative acts and can be made even more dramatic without these acts of civil disobedience by such devices as carrying a coffin, wearing war masks, and using a mule (as did the Poor People's Campaign). Violence is the least justifiable and least effective way to attract attention.

5. *The cooptation argument: poor sociology*

Not only conservative segments of the public, provincial local authorities, and unprofessional police forces oppose peaceful demonstration and further institutionalization of this mode of political expression. It is argued, from the left in the name of Herbert Marcuse, that the kind of tolerance for protest we favor will " coopt " it, and thus reduce the pressures toward necessary social change. The " establishment," it is being said, can learn to "live with " peaceful demonstrations and can, therefore, avoid dealing with the issues for which the demonstrations are organized.[43] With an

---

[43] David Dellinger, the editor of *Liberation*, writes :

" Today non-violence is being challenged, very properly, by people who say it is useful up to a certain point but that it is not a method for social change." " The Recognition of Violence," *The Center Magazine*, Vol. I (November 1968), p. 41.

unusual degree of responsiveness to leftist arguments, some "establishment" representatives have suggested that they ought to keep peaceful demonstrations from becoming fully accepted and institutionalized, lest such response drive protest to more extreme forms. Neither the arguments nor the suggestions built on them seem valid.

To fully accept a channel of political expression does not imply the acceptance of the issues advanced by that channel. Thus, Democrats accept the G.O.P. as a legitimate political party without accepting its views and without the Republicans being "coopted" by the Democrats. There is no indication that where Communists are freely allowed to voice their opinions, they have become "coopted" or have even moderated their views. There is more, rather than less, expression of protest in those parts of the country in which peaceful demonstrations are tolerated than in those in which they are not. *The purpose (and expected effect) of fully accepting and facilitating peaceful demonstrations is not to drain protest but rather to provide it with effective channels of communication.* After all, if the expression of protest leads to the desired response, there surely is little reason for violence even by extremists' own tenets. And if protest does not lead to response, its tolerance will not drain protest; on the contrary, other, more extreme forms of protest will tend to become accepted, and additional supporters will be mobilized. Indeed, an "establishment" which seeks to avoid reforms is illadvised to legitimate peaceful demonstrations. Only establishments which are seeking to become more responsive to their constituencies, even if this entails some far-reaching transformation, will benefit from the institutionalization of more effective channels of communication among aggrieved groups, other members of society, and their government.

The value of peaceful demonstrations becomes even clearer when their effects are compared to those instances in which protest involved violence. While repeated peaceful demonstrations have tended to mobilize a significant part of the nation in support of legitimate needs and demands (e.g., the civil rights movement), violence tends to encourage the opposition of almost all of the public toward the group or view espoused. While the public has *some* tolerance for violence which erupts spontaneously when groups with long neglected grievances turn to rioting, the use of deliberate acts of violence —violence as a political strategy—is very likely to draw the full venom of public rejection, a radical right backlash, and powerful government retaliation. The net effect of petite-violence—such as forcing one's way into a faculty meeting, throwing missiles at policemen, random sniping, or dynamiting a few stores—is to antagonize most of the base of support which a cause may have *and* to provoke the public and the polity into effective counter measures.

Some demonstrators do not want, indeed fear, societal responsiveness and reforms; they rather seek to radicalize their members and recruit additional ones. They are quite willing to sacrifice the sympathy of the majority for the radicalization of the few. If in the process they antagonize most Americans, they believe this plays into their hands: it further " ripens " the country for a total revolutionary change. But such a position is not only morally unacceptable but unrealistic; America is not on the verge of a revolution and cannot forcibly " ripen." And, in those countries in which leftist provocations did bring about oppression from the right, this did not prepare the way for a leftist transformation.

In contemporary America, groups who seek redress of legitimate grievances, therefore, have in fact one major choice— between peaceful protest, which may help promote positive reforms, and mindless, apolitical violence. And, the more a society learns to accept peaceful demonstrations *and* to respond to them the less violence it will face. Hence also the importance of keeping the two kinds of demonstrations as distinct as possible; otherwise, peaceful demonstrators incur all the penalties of violent action without reaping the benefits of non-violent demonstrations.

6. *Restoring civil disobedience to its special status*

A major historical reason for the dangerous blurring of the line between peaceful and violent protests in this country today is that more and more groups now avail themselves of the tool of civil disobedience, a political tactic evolved by the civil rights movement in the nineteen fifties.

Civil disobedience includes activities ranging from those which are completely non-violent (e.g., lunch counter sit-ins) to various degrees of obstruction, up to and including the violation of the rights of others (e.g., to free passage into a classroom).[44] By definition, civil disobedience does not entail the use of force or intimidation against others; also by definition, such violent acts are not legal, at least according to local ordinances. Civil disobedience thus falls clearly between peaceful demonstrations and violent acts, and *both its value and dangers emanate from this special interstitial position.*

Civil disobedience is considered—even among many of its proponents—as a measure of last resort. It is to be used when the law that is challenged is clearly illegitimate; when the injustice resulting from its enforcement is grave; when other forms of political expression are, in effect, not available (e.g., an effective right to vote); and when the failure of the authorities to respond to other means of political expression is deep and prolonged. The dangers are that a) civil disobedience will be used ever more readily, even when other modes of political expression have not been exhausted; b) more groups will use this tool under even less deprived and justifiable conditions (e.g., teachers seeking increases in salary); and c) more extreme forms of civil disobedience will be used. This will result in the line between peaceful and violent protest becoming ever less clear with the expression of protest turning all too readily from peaceful demonstrations to mild forms of civil disobedience, to stronger forms, to outright, deliberate acts of viol-

[44] The latter has been referred to as " uncivil disobedience " by Daniel Bell, " Columbia and the New Left," *The Public Interest,* November 13, 1968, p. 72.

ence.[45] (On the Columbia campus, some students made the transition in less than six days.)

Civil disobedience ought to be restored to the status of an exceptional, extreme, moral act, when all else fails. To achieve this, protestors are to be expected to show great restraint in chosing this form of expression. The argument that the government or local police forces do not always exercise such restraint is based on the false assumption that two wrongs right each other. Police brutality and government unresponsiveness must be corrected, but they do not legitimate demonstrators' brutality or turn provocations into effective political tools.

At the same time, the society must provide fully legitimate *and* effective tools of peaceful political expression for all, not just an occasional election. Opportunities for non-violent demonstrations must exist. Otherwise, as has often been the case in other societies, escalating protests and a rigid non-reforming establishment will reinforce each other, jointly destroying the non-violent shield which must protect any civil society.

*   *   *

Before we move on, it should be reiterated that the overwhelming majority of demonstrations in this country begin and end peacefully, and that many of the small proportion of demonstrations which involve violence do so as a result of action by groups other than the demonstrators. This violent proportion can be reduced to an even smaller one by doing everything possible to provide for peaceful demonstrations: by offering as much leeway in local, state, and national laws and regulations as possible, granting greater police protection, and demanding more self-discipline of the demonstrators. All this will amount to *greater institutionalization of peaceful*

---

[45] On the growing acceptance of civil disobedience as a " routine " act, see The Cox Commission, *op. cit.*, p. 25.

demonstrations, further cementing a viable channel of con-
temporary democracy, and set it apart as much as possible
from violent demonstrations, which undermine democratic
politics.[46]

RESPONSIVENESS: THE KEY FACTOR

Our analysis thus far has focused deliberately on the
phenomenon of demonstrations—their dynamics and place in
democratic politics. By following this approach we have taken
the position that part of the causes of violence and the means
for its prevention rests at the level of alternative modes of
political expression. Violence, we implied, does not simply
erupt because the needs of some members of society are not
satisfied or because they are " frustrated " or " alienated " but
also because such needs and feelings find no other effective
way of expressing themselves. The institutionalization of
peaceful demonstrations and their separation from violent
ones are significant ways both of reducing violence and
increasing the effectiveness of peaceful demonstrations as an
avenue of political expression. They are not to replace existing democratic instruments but to complement them. Actually, as we have seen, demonstrations democratize in that they
increase the *equality of political opportunity* by providing a
tool with a built in advantage for those for whom the other
tools of democracy are somewhat unwieldy and, not infre-
quently, relatively inaccessible.

We turn now to the role played by the " underlying "

[46] The importance of " channel " issues is illustrated by the following
finding. Demands to increase student participation in university policy-
making and to affect dormitory regulations ranked higher than Vietnam
or off-campus civil-rights in a study of demonstrations in 860 campuses.
The figures are respectively 61%, 38% and 29%. 61% includes 34%
re dormitory regulations, and 27% *re* policy-making. Based on data
provided by Richard E. Peterson of the Educational Testing Service in
Princeton, New Jersey, 1968.

causes. Demonstrations seek to express protest and voice new social demands which have not been articulated through existing channels of political expression. To put it in basic terms, were there no issues to protest—because all of the needs of the members of society were taken care of—there would be no need for demonstrations. To put it more technically, a society is more responsive the greater the extent to which the needs of more member-groupings are satisfied, and the more responsive it is (all other things being equal) the fewer demonstrations are to be expected. The prevailing liberal conception of group violence is based precisely on this somewhat elementary insight: if the society were to provide everyone with well-paying jobs, good housing, education, and "meaning," there would be no riots, crime, or demonstrations. A full exploration of the assumptions which underlie this rather simple formula would require a full-blown theory of society, an effort we made elsewhere.[47] Here, only very brief comments are necessary.

1. *The intricate relationship of responsiveness to protest*

a. It seems to be a *valid* observation that if *all* the needs of all the members of society were satisfied, there would be no protest, and hence no violence, but no society is, or ever was, responsive to such an extent.

b. It is *incorrect* to argue that a *relative increase* in responsiveness will yield a related decrease in protest and in violence. The groups to whom the society responds least (e.g., Negroes in the Deep South, farm hands) are far less likely to protest or be violent than groups which have gained a *relative* improvement in their status. Several recent studies of participants in riots support this long established sociological rule. Those who participated in riots, on the average, had lived longer in the community, had better educations, higher incomes, and more jobs than those who did not riot. This find-

[47] *The Active Society. op. cit.*

ing is sometimes misinterpreted to imply that extending jobs, housing, etc., is without effect. Such statements disregard the fact that being relatively better off, in a slum context, is not to be well-off at all. Hence, only limited improvements— responses to some needs—will not be effective and may serve merely to whet appetites and arouse frustrations.

c. Next to the absolute size of the reforms introduced, their relative size as compared to expectations aroused and promises made is significant. Given the same amount of reforms, more protest—and ultimately more violence—will erupt the greater the discrepancy between rhetoric and delivery.

d. Social justice must be sought on its own merits; when a community is urged to " buy " it as a peace-keeping mechanism, this basis for legitimating reforms will sooner or later backfire. First, the community will soon realize that, for reasons discussed, the reforms introduced—especially piecemeal ones—will not buy peace. Second, the community will soon figure out that repressing protesting groups by police methods is much less expensive in the short run than introducing basic reforms, and few people can keep as their reference point the long range situation. Hence, campaigns against poverty, illness and prejudice must be justified on the ground they combat social wrongs, and not as devices for law and order. Here ethics and practicality meet: it is both wrong and impossible to sustain public commitments on other grounds.

e. To argue that an increase in a society's responsiveness to grievances of a member group will not necessarily mollify that group is not to maintain that it will be without effects. The effects of increased responsiveness will be greater.

i) *The larger its magnitude*; token " handouts " are often unconvincing, while significant reallocations of assets carry weight.

ii) *The more encompassing and balanced the increase*; education without jobs, jobs without housing, etc., generate tensions of their own.

iii) *The more immediate the delivery*; once the needs of a social group have been articulated, undue delay in reacting to them cancels out part of the positive effects of the increased responsiveness when it occurs.

iv) *The more the delivery exceeds the commitments;* over the last four years we have seen rapid expansion of the politics of over-sell, in which a " molehill " program is promoted as mountainous social reform. The foundations of such over-sell are deep and include American positivism, optimism, and the need to overcome the reluctance of legislatures to support programs realistically described. Moreover, the over-sell will occasionally "work" : it may produce a new law or a winning candidate. Sooner or later, though, it backfires, eroding the credibility of the program, the leadership, and the political institutions. The disappointments and frustrations thus generated then become themselves a source of protest and, ultimately, of violence. After four years of over-sell a return to the Churchillian rhetoric of sweat and tears needed to ensure basic social transformations, or to that of John F. Kennedy ("don't ask what your country . . ."), is strongly recommended. The more our deeds outdistance our promises (to reverse the current trend), the more protest will subside to that founded on real grievances rather than on reactions to pronouncements by ill-advised politicians.

f.   The society cannot, need not, and ought not respond to all of the demonstrators' demands; it must distinguish between those which are legitimate and those which are not. It is, for instance, one thing for mothers of rat-bitten children to demonstrate when funds to fight the rats are reduced, and quite another for policemen to demonstrate against their superiors.

The selection of legitimate demands is more than an abstract moral exercise. Needs which are not considered genuine by the rest of the community, or by large parts of it, cannot receive effective response in a democratic society. Thus, it is the role of the educators, moral leaders, and of the aggrieved groups to convince at least a majority of the community of the legitimacy of their demands—or to modify these demands in the process of trying to do so.

g. If we turn now to consider the responsiveness to needs considered legitimate by the majority, we find that some of them still receive little response. To satisfy these would require sacrifices of position, privilege, or scarce resources or the use of some means of control of which the community does not approve, e.g., the use of federal troops to impose desegregation of schools. If the American people were facing a simple, zero-sum situation in which the total amount of resources was fixed, and awarding some to one group entailed taking away an equal proportion from others, the hope for keeping and maintaining a peaceful political process would be small indeed. But our choices are not so limited. While reallocation in favor of the underprivileged is both needed and possible, other sources of responsiveness must be found. An obvious one is resources that would be generated by a burgeoning economy, especially if it were working at close to full capacity and not being drained by a war.

Responsiveness, within a given pool of resources and pattern of allocation, will be greater the more *creative* and *anticipatory* is the societal leadership. This includes the executive branch, the legislatures, and community leaders as well as those of social movements. This deserves some elaboration.

2. *The role of leadership*

As the radicals see it, lack of responsiveness on the part of the current leadership is not accidental but endemic to the system; it reflects the monopolization of resources by the privileged classes and the control of the society by a small power elite or military-industrial complex. Responsiveness will come only when these are uprooted following a revolution.

We seek to point out that while power relations and class interests do affect the system's responsiveness, *part* of the lack of responsiveness lies in bureaucratic ineptitude, rigidities, ignorance, and failure to communicate and to anticipate. Responsiveness can hence be increased, significantly in our judgment, by reducing the bureaucratization of the system, and by increasing its creativity, information and capacity to anticipate, precisely because these steps would allow more members of the society to gain more satisfaction without an " ultimate " show-down. These measures would allow us to carve more happiness out of the existing mountain of assets. And, demonstrations are a major way to prod bureaucrats into action, by calling the attention of the public to their ineptness and lack of responsiveness.[48]

Political creativity is the capacity to deal with conflicts through the evolution of " third " alternatives more acceptable to each of the conflicting parties than the positions which initially led to the conflict. For example, the federal aid to education bill became possible when a formula was advanced which satisfied both the Church and the liberal forces advocating the separation of church and state. In this case, however, the evolution and acceptance of the " third " alternative took almost a generation. Similarly, New York City subway, newspaper, and school strikes have been notoriously long. In part this is due to the apparent need to " tire out " the sides until they are weary enough to accept a compromise, but in part it is due to lack of imagination, inventiveness, and leadership of the representatives and intermediaries involved. Creativity *cannot* resolve all conflicts, but it can reduce their scope, shorten their duration, and reduce their costs.

Next, there is a need for the free flow of relatively accurate social *information*. When this is lacking, what the authorities consider to be a response may often not be conceived as such by the demonstrating group. In a major mid-western city, the white leaders decided to respond to unrest in a black neigh-

---

[48] This point was made and a study made of the forces involved in a Latin-American context by Albert O. Hirschman in *Journeys Toward Progress* (Garden City, New York: Doubleday. 1965).

borhood by building, at the city's expense, a large swimming pool, in the neighborhood. The neighborhood spokesmen were very angry—first, because the act was "paternalistic;" the residents had wanted to participate in shaping the response, and were alienated because they were not given this opportunity. Second, they would have preferred a different course of action. Participation is the best way for those in charge to determine the real needs. In this case, the neighborhood badly wanted and needed day-care centers so mothers could work. Several could have been provided for the cost of the pool. In general, a major obstacle to greater responsiveness is sluggishness in the upward flow of social information.

Finally, the capacity to *anticipate*—the cultivation of which the British aristocracy is often credited with and which the French ruling class is said to have lacked—plays another auxiliary role. In part, all action is a contest of power. As the relative power of groups changes significantly, some adjustments in policies, allocations, and institutions are often inevitable although they tend to be resisted by those who are privileged by (or simply accustomed to) existing patterns. The existing leadership is often aware that undue delays in accommodation are explosive, but *because power cannot be assessed accurately*, the leadership tends to overestimate its own and underestimate that of rising groups.

Political action often occurs at this point to "prove" the new power realities. Elections provide a measure of the shift; petitions serve this function as well; and so do demonstrations —by the number of participants and their persistence. None is an accurate criterion and all of them are given to varying degrees of falsification. Still, they are all useful in communicating the reallocation of power. Violence is more likely to result the longer such a shift is ignored and the greater the imbalance before the power shift is adequately taken into account. And anticipation itself helps to maintain the fluidity of the political structure. It should be noted that this kind of anticipation is *not* a device for the maintenance of the *status quo*; the accommodations which result from such anticipation often accumulate to result in the fundamental transformation of the society—e.g., Britain from an aristocratic to a bureaucratic society and the United States from an agrarian to an industrial one. But the transformation is more peaceful the *earlier* the inevitable accommodations are made.

3. *Participation*

Much more can be said and much needs to be learned about the factors which make one polity more creative, informed, and anticipatory than another, but such a discussion would take us far afield indeed. We can only state, without documenting our proposition here, that authentic participation in decision-making by genuine representatives of the " rising " groups is a major way to encourage the presence of all three attributes, and that, difficult as they are to ensure, political systems " short " on them are less responsive and more prone to violence. Peaceful demonstrations serve both as a warning that the extension of participation to some groups is overdue *and* as a stopgap channel for such participation.

First, it must be taken into account that participation in non-violent democratic politics, in conflicts which are limited by rules, does not come "naturally." The citizenry and its leaders must acquire tolerance for others' viewpoints and needs, and the capacity to advance a cause without threatening the basic societal bonds.

" Background " factors affect the *potential* of individuals to acquire the skills of participation in non-violent politics. Studies show that democracy thrives in countries with high levels of education and income *per capita*. People who are malnourished or unable to read and write rarely make good participants in a democratic polity. Hence, the need to improve the basic conditions of life must not be ignored. Second, citizenship education (of the kind once provided to immigrants) and leadership training might help in this regard. To illustrate: one such program is provided by the Scholarship, Education and Defense Fund for Racial Equality. It provides a guide book to be used in the black community to teach local action groups " when to negotiate and how to negotiate, the strategy to be used, the mistakes to be avoided." The need to bargain from strength was stressed, as was the necessity that promises be realistic to avoid undue disappointment with the results. The importance of "coolness" was emphasized: "controlled anger . . . is almost always more effective in negotiations than shouted anger."[49]

Even though such training programs might seem to provide one side in a political conflict with a unilateral advantage, at best they serve to correct existing imbalances, in situations in which relevant skills are already in the possession of representatives of the white middle-class. Moreover, the main effect of a lack of skill in negotiation is to encourage those who suffer from such deficiencies to act in the section of the political arena in which these skills are less necessary, especially to demonstrate. Furthermore, it should be noted that the skills such training programs stress include the desirability of being informed, of knowing the limits of the concessions the other group can be expected to make, and the necessity of keeping "cool," of preventing a situation from exploding unnecessarily. Effective participation in democratic politics requires both knowledge and skill to maintain the conflict without escalating it to a level beyond which the system cannot be maintained. (Of course, those who seek to destroy the community, or are so neglected and rejected by it that they feel it is impossible to transform it into a responsive society, will follow the opposite tack.)

Most important, "background" and "training" notwithstanding, actual participatory experience, as de Tocqueville pointed out long ago, is the best school for democratic politics. In de Tocqueville's day this was chiefly a matter of taking part in town meetings and local politics. Today, participation on the national level is at least as important. Demonstrations provide one such avenue because they either gain national

[49] New York Times, September 22, 1968.

attention (March at Selma) or are national in scope of mobilization (March on Washington) or take place simultaneously across the nation (various anti-war demonstrations). And, hence, partaking in demonstrations related to national issues is a major contemporary way to gain a participatory experience in our democracy.

Participation is also relevant to a particularly difficult aspect of protest, its " expressive " foundation. Several social scientists have distinguished between the specific causes advanced by a group (e.g., open housing) and general, overall issues (e.g., a change in the quality of American life, or " more dignity "). The first kind of demand is referred to as *instrumental*; these issues are viewed as being rational, specific, and involving " means " to a generally agreed-upon end. The second type is considered *expressive* of the general predispositions of the persons or groups which advance them.[50] The underlying assumption is that expressive issues are nonrational and cannot be handled because of their vagueness and lack of specificity, that even when specific demands are met, a group will still protest and may well demonstrate because what it is " really after " is not the specific but a " general " change of status.

There is an element of truth in this analysis, but it neglects two very relevant matters: the relation between instrumental and expressive issues, and the effect of participation. It is a valid observation that when a group is aggrieved in a general way, and, let us say, it becomes enraged over the fact that garbage is collected only once a week as opposed to almost daily garbage collection on Fifth Avenue, sending garbage trucks to the slum neighborhood may well result in the group's shifting to some other specific grievance. But it does not follow that if one specific legitimate grievance after another is corrected, such actions would be without *expressive* effects. On the contrary, we suggest that one of the most effec-

[50] J. Q. Wilson, " Why we are having a wave of violence," *New York Times Magazine*, May 19, 1968.

tive ways to handle expressive protest is to attend to a series of specific issues—as a way of demonstrating a new general orientation. This is especially effective when the specific actions are introduced consistently and openly as indicators of a new orientation. (In this way, for example, John F. Kennedy changed the shape of Soviet-American relations following his Strategy-for-Peace speech.)

Second, and even more significant, there are ways to respond directly to expressive needs, especially through the fostering of participation, in addition to, of course, rather than instead of responding to specific legitimate needs. When we study the history of the pacification of violent conflicts—in cases as different as the turning of two armies into two political parties in Uruguay and the almost complete elimination of violence in management-labor relations[51]—we find that in addition to responding to specific needs, groups previously excluded from the body of society ceased to resort to violence and society ceased to exercise violence in their control once they were considered full-fledged members, once formal citizenship became full and authentic.

The history of the labor class is the best known example and will serve to illustrate the general dynamics: the working class used to be considered as another " nation," a community geographically and culturally separate from " the society " in much the same way that poor and black people have been considered until recent developments somewhat modified this picture. It is this definition of a group as excluded from society which is used to " justify " violence *on both sides* (as it does in international relations) and the lack of responsiveness to legitimate needs (our sense of responsibility to American poor people, as weak as it is, is much stronger than that to poor people which live across the border, say in Mexico). Historically, the stage at which violence was phased out and responsiveness was increased coincides with the time when

[51] Amitai Etzioni, " On Self-Encapsulating Conflicts," *Journal of Conflict Resolution,* Vol. 8 (1964), pp. 242-255.

the excluded group is allowed to " enter " the society and acquire the symbols of membership and participation. While the analogy to the working class is quite limited in terms of groups to whom the society now only begins to respond, and which are most likely to demonstrate firstly because their capacity to exert economic pressure on the society is small—we suggest that it does hold on this one key point. An effective right to vote, to be elected, to participate in all levels of decision-making, and to share in public ceremonies—in addition to the intrinsic value of such participation as means of sharing in the allocative decisions—all have considerable expressive value.

We would like to stress as strongly as possible that we do not mean that increasing the efficacy of the political process can substitute for genuine responsiveness to material needs, appropriation of resources, sharing of privileges, etc. On the contrary, if " participation " in politics is offered without the sharing of wealth and extension of rights, the final explosion, while its occurrence might be delayed for a while, will be that much larger. Political efficacy is needed to a) meet needs which cannot be answered elsewhere and b) to pave the way for accommodations in other areas, such as economic and social. Just as more jobs, houses, and schools will not in themselves solve the problem of feeling excluded, a feeling of participation will not long suffice, and in the end will boomerang, if it is not combined with a sharing in the wealth and rights of the society.

*   *   *

It has been suggested that violence has frequently preceded major social changes in America, and that often the " establishment " agrees to the necessary changes only when it realized that such response was required if peace and stability were to be maintained. While this is undoubtedly true, the dangers of resorting to this instrument must also be recognized. And, the more we learn to be creative, informed, anticipatory, and participatory, the more we will be able to adjust earlier and to a greater extent and, hence, with less violence.

Ultimately, a society which fails to respond effectively to its members, especially when the neglect of the needs of some of them has been accumulating and has been repeatedly called to its attention, will have little choice except between anarchy and tyranny. Demonstrations are a useful though potentially volatile warning mechanism. Muffling their sound will not prevent the explosion.

APPENDIX A

A Demonstration Month—A list of 216 Incidents

In the following pages, all the incidents of protest which were reported by *The New York Times* and *The Washington Post* during the period of September 16, 1968 to October 15, 1968 are listed. The first right hand score is either O, F, or L which stand respectively for the main target of the demonstration which was an organization (such as a university or church), federal government or a local one. The total distribution is:

O	105	48.61%
F	66	30.55%
L	41	18.98%
NA	4	1.85%
	216	99.99%

The next score—P, V, or O—stands for Peaceful, Violent or Obstructionist. The total distribution is:

P	134	62.03%
V	75	34.72%
O	7	3.24%
	216	99.99%

For methodological discussion see **Appendix B.**

59

No.	Place	Date	Group	Brief Description		
1.	New York N.Y.	9.15.68	Parents & Teachers	Picket for keeping schools open	P	L
2.	Wash.,D.C.	9.15.68	Catholic laymen	Rally to support ousted priests	P	O
3.	Birmingham, Ala	9.15.68	People	Marched in memory of 4 Negro girls killed	P	?
4.	Baltimore, Md.	9.15.68	Negro crowd	Pelted officers & motorists with bottles etc. 5 arrested	V	O
5.	Toledo, Ohio	9.15.68	Negro gangs	Objects hurled, firebombed supermarket, 21 arrested 4 policemen injured	V	O
6.	Saginaw, Mich.	9.16.68	Negro & Mexican youths	rock-throwing, window smashing foray	V	O
7.	Nyack, N.Y.	9.16.68	Negro youths	broke windows, scuffled with police, 6 arrested	V	O
8.	N.Y., N.Y.	9.16.68	Striking teachers and supporters	Supporting Union walkout	F	L
9.	N.Y., N.Y.	9.16.68	Teachers (mostly white)		P	O
10.	N.Y., N.Y.	9.17.68	Teachers		P	O
11.	N.Y., N.Y.	9.17.68	Fed. of Puerto Rican Parents		P	O
12.	Brooklyn,N.Y.	9.17.68	Welfare recipients	Overturned furniture, ripped telephones -- barred 600 case-workers from centers	V	L
13.	N.Y., N.Y.	9.17.68	Welfare recipients	Wandered through records & admin. areas of center, disrupting service	P	L
14.	N.Y., N.Y.	9.18.68	Garment Workers U.		P	O
15.	Buffalo, N.Y.	9.17.68	Anti-war students	Political meeting	P	F
16.	Buffalo, N.Y.	9.17.68	Youngsters (left wing)	Political meeting	P	F

No.	Date	Place	Group	Brief Description	
17.	9.18.68	Phil. Pa.	Mainly white	Marched outside school admin. bldg. protesting busing	P L
18.	9.18.68	Chicago Ill.	High Sch.Students Negro & white	15 injured, 9 suspended -- fighting in hall-ways, 5 juveniles, 2 adults arrested -- bricks thrown at police cars after school	V O
19.	9.18.68	St. Joe, Mich	Welfare mothers	4 persons 2 policemen injured in scuffle	V L
20.	9.18.68	N.Y., N.Y.	Students	Block doorway to registration, seized guards' clubs, students thrown, etc.	V O
21.	9.18.68	N.Y., N.Y.	Students	Defied a Univ. order, invaded bldg. marched around campus	P O
22.	9.18.68	Fresno,Cal.	Mex-Ameri. grape pickers & support.	Political meeting	P F
23.	9.18.68	San Fran.	Anti-war Students	Political meeting	P F
24.	9.18.68	Kansas C. Mo.	Anti-Wallace	Mostly shouting, 1 fist fight, supporters threw cups, dozen hecklers taken from hall by police	V F
25.	9.18.68	Univ.Pk, Pa.	Students		P O
26.	9.18.68	Teaneck, NJ	Youthful Negroes	Marched through streets - broken windows	V L
27.	9.18.68	Wash.,D.C.	NA	Attended sch. Bd. Meeting cheered adoption of neighborhood school control projects	P L
28.	9.18.68	Brooklyn, NY	Black Panthers	Attended court hearing of Black Panther leader wearing buttons with slogans such as "Black Power" etc.	P L
29.	9.19.68	Canadaiqua, NY	Anti-war demonst.		P F
30	9.19.68	N.Y., NY	Cuban refugees	3 smoke bombs set off at theatre - pro-Castro Play, no injuries	V ?
31.	9.19.68	Boston, Mass	Anti-War demonst.	Political meeting	P F
32.	9.19.68	N.Y., NY	Students		P O

No.	Place	Date	Group	Brief Description		
33	New York, NY	9.19.68	Demonstrators	Bottles etc. at police, 3 policemen slightly injured, 2 demonstrators to custody	V	L
34	L. A., Calif.	9.20.63	Spectators, hippies	Board of Regents-Reagan's opposition to Cleaver teaching a course on campus	P	O
35	Beltsville, Md.	9.19.63	Union Members	Union picketing Co. offices, Nephew Co. owner arrested, charged with assaulting Union plant supervisor	V	O
36	New York, NY	9.20.63	75 persons	To show support for Ocean Hill-Brownsville school board	P	O
37	NYC to Albany, NY	9.20.68	Parents & Children		P	L
38	Brooklyn, NY	9.20.63	Teachers & Parents		P	L
39	Titusville, Fla	9.20.68	Negro & white youths	Fighting, 7 injured inc. 3 police, 5 Negroes, 5 whites arrested Ft. ball game Negro Youths - school bandsmen played "Dixie" Negroes began beating them.	V	O
40	Orlando, Fla.	9.20.68	Negro & white youths	Game between largely Negro & largely white school stones at motorists, skirmishes, 4 hospitalized	V	O
41	Montgomery, Ala.	9.20.68	Youths + 1 black wo. 1 black teen	Wallace supporter slapped black youth, another knocked a youth down & a policeman jumped on his back	V	F
42	Montgomery City Md.	9.21.68	Residents	County for scrapping proposal to build low cost housing	P	L
43	Sussex, Va.	9.19.68	High School Students		P	O
44	New York, NY	9.16.68	Trade Unionists		P	O
45	New York, NY	9.21.68	Community Residents		P	O
46	Boston, Mass.	9.21.68	Antiwar Protesters	Political meeting	P	F

No.	Place	Date	Group	Brief Description	
47	Wash., D. C.	9.22.68	Catholics (assume)		P O
48	Rockville, Md.	9.22.68	Catholics (assume)		P O
49	Bethesda, Md.	9.22.63	Catholics (assume)		P O
50	Wash., D. C.	9.22.68	Catholics (assume)		P O
51	Rockville, Md.	9.22.63	Catholics (assume)		P O
52	Wash., D. C.	9.22.68	Catholic		P O
53	Cleveland, Ohio	9.22.63	AntiWar Youths	Political Meeting	P F
54	Euclid Beach Pk., Ohio	9.22.68	AntiWar Youths	Political meeting	P F
55	New York, NY	9.22.68	20 Negroes	For not representing the causes/aspirations of black people	P O
56	Milwaukee, Wisc.	9.22.63	Catholics Antiwar	Disrupted mass, rushed to altar, scuffled with priest, 3 arrested, tried to read statement urging church to 'resist war & racism'	V O
57	Chicago, Ill.	9.18.68	White parents	An integrated plan for schools (Inc. busing) ordered by Court	P L
58	Pittsburgh, Pa.	9.22.68	1 Negro Prisoner	Protesting for self and 30 Negro inmates	P O
59	Baltimore, Md.	9.23.63	NA Union members		P O
60	Berkeley, Calif.	9.23.63	2 Yippies		P F
61	Syracuse, NY	9.23.68	Negro youths	Firebomb 4 local stores, tear gas, 7 Negro youths arrested, 1 white man into custody-- possession of weapon	V O
62	Syracuse, NY	9.21.68	Groups (Assume Negro)	Rocks hurled at police, 3 police injured, suspicious fire, 3 arrested	V O
63	Milwaukee, Wisc.	9.23.63	Many Voters	Political meeting	P F

No.	Place	Date	Group	Brief Description		
64	Wash., D. C.	9.21.68	Prison inmates	Broke chairs, set mattresses on fire, threw debris at guards	V	O
65	York, Pa.	9.23.68	High School Students		P	O
66	New York, NY	9.23.63	Union workers		P	L
67	Newark, NJ	9.23.63	Welfare Recipients	Sit-in blocked access to offices, shoving of welfare workers	V	L
68	Jersey City, NJ	9.24.63	3 Black Panthers	Blocking Traffic, refused to move, assaulted officers	V	O
69	Waycross, Ga.	9.24.63	Negro Pub. School Students		P	O
70	Louisville, Ky.	9.24.63	Crowd of Negroes	4 or 5 shots fired at police cars amid racial disorder--cars hit	V	O
71	Louisville, Ky.	9.23.68	Negroes (mostly)	Racial outbreak, fireman shot, wounded while dousing burning auto	V	O
72	Milwaukee, Wisc.	9.24.63	Peace Protesters Inc. 5 Cath. priests	Broke into selective service office, scattered, burned records, 14 arrested	V	F
73	Syracuse, NY	9.24.68	Negro youths	Bottles thrown, cars stolen, overturned, set afire, 5 injured	V	O
74	Seattle, Wash.	9.24.63	AntiWar Protesters	Political meeting	P	F
75	New York, NY	9.24.68	Anti-Castro Cubans	Picketed pro-Castro play, some battled with police, 6 arrested	V	?
76	York, Pa.	9.24.68	Street gangs	2nd night, terrorized citizenry, isolated incidents of violence, 1 man seriously injured by small band of Negroes, no arrests	V	O
77	Anne Arundel Co. Md.	9.20.68	Negro & White Youths	Football game disorder, teacher hospitalized, student cut, no arrest	V	O
78	New Orleans, La.	9.23.68	Policemen's wives		P	L

No.	Place	Date	Group	Brief Description		
79	Binghamton, NY	9.25.68	College age people		P	F
80	Trenton, NJ	9.25.68	High School Students	Racial Protesting attacks by Negro students	P	O
81	Trenton, NJ	9.24.68	Negro High School Students	Roughed up white students	V	O
82	Trenton, NJ	9.24.68	Negro High School Students		P	L
83	New York, NY	9.25.68	Parents		P	L
84	Washington, Pa.	9.25.68	AntiWar Students		P	F
85	Denver, Colo.	9.24.68	Negro Youths	Invasions of High School grounds, assaults on White Students	V	O
86	New York, NY	9.25.68	SDS Students		P	O
87	Montclair, NJ	9.26.68	Negro High School Students		P	O
88	Bethesda, Md.	9.26.63	High School Students	Culminating days of conflict, dissident youth knocked unconscious	V	O
89	Bethesda, Md.	9.25.68	High School Students	Dissident Group with black arm bands rally around black flag in quadrangle, taunted and pushed by anti-protesters	V	O
90	Bethesda, Md.	9.24.63	High School Students		P	O
91	Waterbury, Conn.	9.26.68	White High School Students		P	O
92	New York, NY	9.26.68	Parents, Teachers and Supervisors		P	L
93	Brooklyn, NY	9.26.68	Women	Threw chairs, attempted block doors, 2 arrested	V	L
94	Boston, Mass.	9.25.68	Negro Youths	Bottles at police, supermarket looted, 3 stores robbed, 12 injured following black power rally	V	O

No.	Place	Date	Group	Brief Description		
95	Boston, Mass.	9.26.68	Negro youths	Rocks at police & cars driven by whites, a fire bombing, 8 police injured	V	O
96	Detroit, Mich.	9.26.63	College students	Political meeting	P	F
97	New York, NY	9.26.68	Teachers		P	O
98	New York, NY	9.26.68	Students	Rally crowd into street toward church, met police 3 arrested, several clubbed, returned campus, rocks at Cordier's office	V	O
99	New York, NY	9.26.63	S.D.S. Reps		O	O
100	Philadelphia, Pa.	10.14.68	High School Students		P	O
101	Trenton, NJ	9.26.68	White High School Students		P	O
102	Portland Oregon	9.27.68	AntiWar protesters	Political meeting	P	F
103	Long Island, NY	9.27.68	Demonstrators		P	F
104	Rochester, NY	9.27.68	Union Members		P	O
105	Waterbury, Conn.	9.27.68	White High School Students	Boycotted classes, protest rally in park, skirmishes with Negroes, 2 injured	V	O
106	Waterbury, Conn.	9.25.68	Negro High School Students		P	O
107	New York, NY	9.27.68	'Radical' Students		P	O
108	New York, NY	9.27.68	Brooklyn Residents		P	L
109	Brooklyn, NY	9.27.68	Teachers & supporters	Teachers & students tried unsuccessfully to cross picket line, scuffles resulted	V	L
110	Baltimore, Md.	9.23.63	Union members		P	O
111	Baltimore, Md.	10.9.63	Demonstrators		P	F

No.	Place	Date	Group	Brief Description		
112	Chicago, Ill.	9.27.68	Negro Teenagers	Rocks at police, stormed buses, terrorized passengers, robbed 2 drivers, fireman & policeman cut	V	O
113	Aurora, Ill.	9.27.68	Youths	Stoned buses after football game	V	O
114	Trenton, NJ	9.27.68	Youngsters	Broke number of car windows, predominantly Negro area	V	O
115	New York, NY	9.27.68	Yippies		P	F
116	Chicago, Ill.	9.28.68	Whites		P	L
117	New York, NY	10.10.68	Teachers & pupils		P	O
118	Wash., DC	9.29.68	Catholics		P	O
119	New York, NY	10.9.68	Students & CORE Leader		P	L
120	Chicago, Ill.	9.29.68	"United Patriots International"		P	F
121	Wash., DC	9.29.68	Protesters		P	F
122	Seattle, Wash.	9.28.68	AntiWar	Political meeting	P	F
123	Sarasota, Fla.	9.29.68	Negroes	Rock throwing crowd broken with tear gas, regrouped in bands, stoned cars etc. 10 arrested	V	O
124	Newark, NJ	9.29.68	Prison inmates	178 men ordered into cells, refused, rioted, broke windows fires	V	O
125	Falls Church, Va.	9.30.68	Community Residents		P	L
126	Wash., DC	10.1.68	Students		P	O
127	Prince Geo. Co. Md.	9.30.68	Housewives		P	L
128	Chicago, Ill.	9.30.68	Wallaceites & AntiWar	Brief scuffle between a white man and Negro, Police quickly separated groups	V	F

No.	Place	Date	Group	Brief Description	
129	New York, NY	9.30.68	Students		P L
130	New York, NY	9.30.68	Welfare Patrolmen		P L
131	Brooklyn, NY	9.30.63	Puerto Rican Parents		P O
132	Brooklyn, NY	9.30.63	Black Teachers		P L
133	Brooklyn, NY	10.1.68	Teachers, parents children	Protesters caused closing of three schools-- melees with police, 9 arrested, 10 police injured	V O
134	Erie, Pa.	10.1.68	AntiWar protesters youths, Wallaceites	Political meeting	P F
135	Wash., DC	10.1.68	Yippies		P F
136	New York, NY	10.1.68	University Employees		P O
137	Fort Dix, NJ	10.1.68	AntiWar protesters		P F
138	Grand Rapids, Michigan	10.1.68	Students	A number of scuffles, no injuries	V F
139	Flint, Mich.	10.1.63	Dissenters	Political meeting	P F
140	Columbus, SC	10.1.68	Prisoners	Attacked guards, set fires, smashed furniture, 5 injured	V O
141	Elizabeth, NJ	10.1.63	Negro High School Students		P O
142	Baltimore, Md.	10.2.63	Members of 5 unions		P O
143	Baltimore, Md.	10.2.63	AFTRA members		P O
144	Zion, Ill.	10.2.68	Negro & White High School Students	Fighting between Negro & White, clubbed resisting police, Negro taken into custody, rocked police car	V O
145	Norfolk, Va.	10.2.68	Youths	Political meeting	P F

No.	Place	Date	Group	Brief Description		
146	Elizabeth NJ	10.2.68	Negro Students		P	O
147	New York N.Y.	19.2.68	"Youth Against War and Fascism"		P	F
148	Canton, Ohio	10.2.68	Young Negroes	Political Meeting	P	F
149	New York N.Y.	10.3.68	Hippie types	Series of street disorders, bricks at police, fires in trash cans, 9 arrested, 4 police injured	V	L
150	Bronx, N.Y.	10.3.68	Parents		P	L
151	Portland, Ore.	10.3.68	Young dissidents		P	F
152	Wash. D.C.	10.3.68	Anti-war Yippies		P	F
153	Wash. D.C.	10.4.68	Catholics (assume)		P	O
154	Wash. D.C.	10.4.68	Students		P	O
155	Spokane Wash.	10.4.68	Young dissenters		P	F
156	Columbus S.C.	10.4.68	Wallace supporters	Political Meeting	P	F
157	Hartford, Conn.	10.4.68	Young people Students	Political Meeting	P	F
158	L. A. Calif	10.4.68	Students & SDS		P	F
159	New York N.Y.	10.4.68	H.Sch.Students & supporters	Battled with police, 9 police injured, at least 8 adults and 4 youths into custody	V	L
160	New York N.Y.	10.4.68	Community Group		O	L
161	Pittsburgh Pa.	10.2.68	Negro young.	Scuffles - apparently Negro-White	V	F
162	Toledo, Ohio	10.3.68	Hecklers, Negro Students, Mid-class	Man struck in head by stone thrown from group of hecklers	V	F

No.	Place	Date	Group	Brief Description	
163	Buffalo N.Y.	10.5.68	Wh.Students Mid-Class, Negroes	Scuffles--shots fired into downtown stores White Anti-Wallace demonstrators roamed streets after rally	V F
164	Indianapolis Ind.	10.3.68	Hecklers	Hecklers scuffled 3 times with Wallace supporters 4 arrested	V F
165	Newark N.J.	10.5.68	Protesters	Minor scuffles, a negro emerged with bloody face	V F
166	Cleveland Ohio	10.5.68	Demonstrators	Scuffling between demonstrators and police between black and white, several injured, 6 arrested	V F
167	Minneapolis Minn.	9.30.68	Students		P O
168	Memphis, Tenn.	10.5.68	Hospital Workers		P L
169	Columbus S.C.	10.5.68	Prison inmates	Rioted, furniture tossed, 2 small fires tear gas used	V O
170	Boston, Mass.	10.6.68	People		P F
171	Knoxville,Tenn.	10.2.68	Students	Political meeting	P F
172	Baltimore Md.	10.7.68	Demonstrators	Some minor scuffles with group of counter demonstrators	V F
173	Syracuse N.Y.	10.7.68	Students	Political meeting	P F
174	Baltimore Md.	10.7.68	Priests, Hippies Peace protesters	Minor scuffles, several hundred demonstrators moved toward exits some refused to leave, 5-8 arrests	V F
175	Washington DC.	10.7.68	Picketers		P O
176	Baltimore Md.	10.8.68	Demonstrators		P F
177	Wash. D.C.	10.8.68	Demonstrators	Political meeting	P F
178	Brooklyn N.Y.	10.8.68	Community Residents mostly Negro		P L
179	Boston Mass.	10.8.68	Hecklers, mostly young, students	Political meeting	P F

No.	Place	Date	Group	Brief Description		
180	Wash. D.C.	10.8.68	Young Negroes	Erupted after protest rally related to H. St. shooting, broken windows, 1 major fire, 1 arrest, tear gas used.	V	L
181	Chicago Ill.	10.9.68	Negro & Puerto H. Sch.Students	3rd day of walk-out, police clear building--eight minor fires broken windows	V	O
182	Chicago Ill.	10.9.68	Negro H.SchStudents		P	O
183	Chicago Ill	10.8.68	Students mostly Negro	15 arrests--demonstrations at four schools--some were white, protesting Negro demands.	P	O
184	Brooklyn N.Y.	10.9.68	Parents,Children Supporters P.Ricans	Clashes between police and demonstrators, man clubbed, 2 police injured trying to move crowd from intersection 7 arrested	V	O
185	Brooklyn N.Y.	10.9.68	Teenagers & adults many Negro		P	O
186	Baltimore Md.	10.9.68	Demonstrators		P·	F
187	Santa Mon.Cal.	10.9.68	Young People Peace & Freedom party	Political meeting	P	F
188	New York N.Y.	10.9.68	Young people	21 arrested, 10 injured--clash came when police tried to move barricades toward sidewalk.	V	F
189	New York N.Y.	10.9.68	Prof.Social Workers	Blocked entrance, public property, 34 arrested peacefully	O	L
190	Gary, Ind.	10.9.68	Sanitation Workers		P	L
191	Phil. Pa.	10.9.68	Whites, assume H. School Students	Gathered around largely Negro school harrass students going home.	P	O
192	Akron, Ohio	10.10.68	Students		P	F
193	Baltimore Md.	10.10.68	Mostly young		P	F
194	Scranton Pa.	10.9.68	Sch-age hecklers	2 teen-aged girls shoved, led out by police.	V	F

No.	Place	Date	Group	Brief Description		
195	Towson, Md.	10.11.68	Students	Political Meeting	P	F
196	New York N.Y.	10.11.68	Students	Barricaded 2 buildings--after concessions by university, marched out peacefully.	0	0
197	New York N.Y.	10.11.68	Students		P	0
198	Denver, Colo.	10.11.68	Mostly Students	Several scuffles as the campaign audience dispersed	V	F
199	Phil. Pa.	10.11.68	Negro Youths	Invaded a morning assembly at a High Sch. 4 wh. 3 Negro injured	V	0
200	Wash. D.C.	10.9.68	Cafeteria Workers		P	F
201	Newark N.J.	10.11.68	Students & Puerto Ricans & supporters		P	0
202	Wash. D.C.	10.12.68	Mostly Negro	Rally to protest 14th st. shooting, poured into street-- blocked off traffic area with rented truck	0	L
203	San.Fran. Cal.	10.12.68	G.I.Reservists Veterans & Civilians		P	F
204	Annapolis Md.	10.12.68	Youths Negro neighborhood	Started after arrest of young man and girl fighting, rock throwing looted 1 shop, minor fires 2 stores, barricaded street, 2 other arrests, no injuries.	V	0
205	Wash. D.C.	10.13.68	(Assume) Negroes	After concert hurled bricks, windows broken, teenage gangs, 4 arrested, 3 police injured, tear gas.	V	0
206	San Fran.Cal.	10.13.68	Peace & Freedom Pty. supporters	Several scuffles, no arrests.	V	F
207	Wash. D.C.	10.14.68	Young people, assume Negroes	Police sealed off area when young went on a window breaking, looting spree, 2 arrested, tear gas	V	?
208	New York N.Y.	10.14.68	Univ. Employees & Students	Employees stage sit-in, student supporters massed outside, sit-ins emerged, students dispersed peacefully.	0	0

No.	Place	Date	Group	Brief Description		
209	Cummins Prison Farm, Ark.	10.14.68	Prison inmates	Inmates staged sit-down work strike, guards wounded 24 with shotguns to force them back to work.	V	O
210	Santa Bar.Cal.	10.14.68	Black Student Union	Seized classroom, locked themselves in with Dean of Students gave up peacefully when university acceded to some demands	O	O
211	San Diego Cal.	10.14.68	Hecklers, young adults	Political meeting	P	F
212	New York N.Y.	10.13.68	Students	2 bombs exploded, fire hoses and telephone wires cut, locks damaged, toilets plugged	V	O
213	New York N.Y.	10.14.68	Students		P	O
214	New York N.Y.	10.14.68	Parents, Teachers Students		P	L
215	New York N.Y.	10.14.68	Striking Teachers	Picketed outside school, some youngsters threw erasers at them	V	O
216	Chicago Ill.	10.14.68	Negro Youngsters (students)	Joined in boycotting H.Schods, fires reported set at some, false fire alarms emptied classrooms at others.	V	O

APPENDIX B

Methodological Notes

1. Our figures are based solely on the articles in *The New York Times* and *The Washington Post* as we found them. This is not to imply that we question the newspapers' accuracy, consistency, or completeness of reporting, but rather that we had neither the time nor the facilities to verify their statements, nor to study other papers. Such a focus obviously affected our discussion. Events which occurred in Washington and New York, which involved large numbers of people, and which led to violence or were particularly dramatic in some way, are probably over-represented. What we show, therefore, is a *rough approximation* of the frequency of demonstrations and the number and range of their participants and not a statistically valid or reliable measurement.

It should be noted that the effect of this data on our conclusions is to make them more conservative in two ways: the data under-estimates the number of demonstrations which occurred and makes them seem less peaceful than they probably actually were.

2. It might be argued that the selection of a month so close to a Presidential election inflates the total number of demonstrations, and this argument has some merit. However, it is indicative of the general trend toward more demonstrations that many more are recorded in the month at hand than, we expect, occurred in the same month in 1964 or 1960, not to mention earlier election years. Second, it is difficult to conceive of a " typical " month. The choice of a month in the spring might well overrepresent demonstrations on university

and college campuses, and "the long, hot summers" generate their own "atypical" situations. Third, we excluded from our count articles which merely mentioned that "a few hecklers were present" when a candidate spoke. We included the heckling of candidates only when it seemed to be the action of an organized group for a specific purpose, a group which might well have protested elsewhere had there not have been an election.

3. We studied demonstrations, as deliberate acts of protest, but not riots, which we consider spontaneous events. We included disturbances only if they followed a specific incident which they sought to protest (as distinct from those which draw only on a general alienation). But even if we had included riots our figures would not have changed much as there were only a few during the period studied.

4. Each incident of demonstration was counted separately even if several demonstrations were carried out by the same group with the same goal—e.g., SDS demonstrating against the war in Vietnam several times over the course of the month would be counted as several incidents. On the other hand, reports of "looting in several parts of the city" in response to a particular event were considered one demonstration. The same holds for a single incident which lasted more than one day.

5. Labor strikes and activities were not counted as demonstrations unless they involved "irregular" activities such as picketing in the streets. The same rule was followed for political meetings.

6. When a demonstration was initially peaceful and then became obstructionist or violent, it was scored as obstructionist or violent rather than peaceful. In other words, while the sequence of escalation of demonstrations would in itself be an interesting and important topic of study, here a demonstration was classified by its highest level of escalation.

We are unsatisfied with the amount of data we could collect as well as with the extent of checking and cross-checking possible under the circumstances. Those familiar with the time and costs involved in research of this sort will understand our predicament if we state that this study had to be carried out in less than two months, with a total budget of $2,000.

The Author, Amitai Etzioni, is Professor of Sociology at Columbia University and a member of the Institute of War and Peace Studies in New York. His books include *A Comparative Analysis of Complex Organizations* (The Free Press, 1961), *Political Unification* (Holt, Rinehart and Winston, 1965), and *The Active Society* (The Free Press, 1968). He is the director of the Center for Policy Research. His main interests are social and political theory, and domestic and international organizations. He has written widely for professional journals, popular magazines, *The New York Times,* and *The Washington Post.* Professor Etzioni received two Faculty Fellowships from the Social Science Research Council and was a Fellow of the Center for Advanced Study in the Behavioral Sciences at Stanford. He is a member of the editorial boards of the *American Sociological Review, Administrative Science Quarterly,* and *Sociological Inquiry.* He has recently been appointed to the Committee on Professional Ethics of the American Sociological Association.

Professor Etzioni received his Ph.D. from the University of California at Berkeley in 1958 and his M.A. in 1956 from The Hebrew University in Jerusalem.

ACKNOWLEDGEMENTS

The coding of newspaper clippings was carried out by Miss Beth Zeidman, under the supervision of Miss Sarajane Heidt and the author. The author is indebted for comments on a previous draft of this paper to Martin Wenglinsky as well as Sarajane Heidt, Carolyn O. Atkinson and Murray Milner, all on the staff of the Center for Policy Research. I am grateful to Mary Helen Shortridge for editorial suggestions.

APPENDIX C

COMMISSION STATEMENT ON GROUP VIOLENCE

DR. MILTON S. EISENHOWER, *Chairman*

DECEMBER, 1969

National Commission on
the Causes and Prevention of Violence

I

Causes: Historical and Comparative Aspects

We tend to think of group violence[1] as a major aberration in a democratic society, as a sickness that comes only in extraordinary times. A deeper reading of the past belies this notion. In man's political history, group violence has accompanied periods of serious social stress from Homer to this morning's newspaper. Group violence runs through the American experience, as it always has, in varying degrees and manifestations, for every society. Violence has been used by groups seeking

[1] For present purposes we define group violence as the unlawful threat or use of force by any group that results or is intended to result in the injury or forcible restraint or intimidation of persons, or the destruction or forcible seizure of property.

79

power, by groups holding onto power, and by groups in the process of losing power. Violence has been pursued in the defense of order by the satisfied, in the name of justice by the oppressed, and in fear of displacement by the threatened.

At the outset, it must be made clear that group violence has no necessary relationship to group protest, although there continue to be those who decry the one as though it were the other. The right to protest is an indispensable element of a free society; the exercise of that right is essential to the health of the body politic and its ability to adapt itself to a changing environment. In this country, we have endowed the right of protest with constitutional status. The very first Amendment to the Constitution protects freedom of speech and press and " the right of the people peaceably to assemble and to petition the Government for a redress of grievances." The Amendment protects much more than the individual right of dissent; it guarantees the right of groups to assemble and petition, or, in the modern phrase, to demonstrate.

Group violence, on the other hand, is dangerous to a free society. All too frequently, it is an effort not to persuade, but to compel. It has no protected legal status; indeed, one purpose of law is to prevent and control it. Nor is group violence a necessary consequence of group protest. The violence of the Ku Klux Klan—the lynching of Negroes at the rate of almost 100 per year from 1890 to 1910—had little to do with protest; if anything, it was more a cause of protest than a response. The same may be said of the harsh treatment of Orientals on the Pacific frontier and the common use of violence to settle property and political disputes among competing groups in the early days of the American West.

It is true, of course, that group protest sometimes results in group violence. Violence may be committed by groups opposed to the aims of the protesters (as in the Southern murders of civil rights workers by groups of white militants); excessive force may be used by the public authorities, as in Selma in 1965; violence may be committed by some within the protesting group itself (as in the case of the Weatherman faction of the SDS). But the widely held belief that protesting groups usually behave violently is not supported by fact. Of the multitude of occasions when protesting groups exercise their rights of assembly and petition, only a small number result in violence.

Thus, our Task Force Report on Historical and Comparative Perspectives on violence reports that over the five-year period from mid-1963 to mid-1968, protests or counter-protests and ghetto riots involved more than 2 million persons. Civil rights demonstrations mobilized 1.1 million, anti-war demonstrations 680,000, and ghetto riots an estimated 200,000. Nine thousand casualties resulted, including some 200 deaths.[2] Ghetto riots were responsible for most of these casualties, including 191 deaths. Almost all other deaths, an estimated 23, resulted from white terrorism against blacks and civil rights workers. These casualty figures are for a five-year period, and apart from the ghetto riots, they are comparatively infinitesimal. While they are not to be condoned, in a country with 250,000 aggravated assaults and 12,000 homicides per year, group protest cannot be considered as accounting for a major part of the deliberate violence we experience.[3]

Do we have a greater amount of group violence today than in earlier periods of our history? While a precise quantitative answer cannot be provided, we may conclude with confidence

[2] Report of the Task Force on Historical and Comparative Perspectives, *Violence in America*, Vol. 2 (U.S. Government Printing Office: Washington, D.C., 1969), pp. 445-6. The Department of Justice recorded 22 deaths in civil disturbances in the last 6 months of 1968 and the first 3 months of 1969; 11 of these deaths occurred in a single disturbance—the Cleveland "shoot-out" in July of 1968. Similarly, while most of the nation's 2,300 college campuses probably experienced some kind of demonstrative protest during the academic year 1968-1969, the American Council on Education has found that only about 6% of the colleges experienced any violence. *Campus Disruption During 1968-1969*, ACE Research Reports, Vol. 4, No. 3 (1969), p. 8.

[3] Comparative figures for property damage as the result of group protests are not available. But when measured against property damage resulting from more than 1,000,000 annual robberies and burglaries reported in crime statistics, it also seems likely that group protest accounts for a very small part of the deliberate property damage we experience.

that, while group violence in the 1960's was at a higher level than in the decades immediately preceding, several earlier decades of American history were marked by higher levels of group violence—in terms of casualties per 100,000 population —than has been true of the decade now ending.

Ever since the Boston Tea Party, occasional group violence has been a recurring—though not a continuous—feature of American political and social history:

● From 1740 to 1790, Appalachian farmers, protesting against debt and tax collectors from the seaboard centers of political and economic power, engaged in a series of violent disorders, of which the Whiskey Rebellion in Pennsylvania is best known.

● Southern landowners and northern Abolitionists engaged in a variety of skirmishes, from " bleeding Kansas " to John Brown's raid on Harper's Ferry, that were the violent prelude to the Civil War.

● During Reconstruction, the Ku Klux Klan and other elements of the defeated white majority in the South conducted a campaign of terrorism against the freed blacks, government officials and Southerners who cooperated with them.

● So-called " Native Americans " of the original colonial stocks resorted to group violence when they perceived their status as threatened by European Catholic and Jewish immigrants in the East and Orientals in the West; the immigrant groups occasionally engaged in violence such as the New York Draft Riots in 1863.

● As the freed Negro migrants from the South began settling in border and Northern cities after the Civil War, white residents (including the most recent of the European immigrants) launched occasional attacks on black sections of the city.

● The growth of organized labor in the half century
from 1880 to 1930 was marked by unusually severe episodes of violence in which employers, workers and public
authorities were all occasional aggressors. In the three-
year period 1902-1904, about 200 persons were killed and
2,000 injured in the violence accompanying various
strikes and lockouts.

During each of these episodes, most of the community con-
tinued to live in peace. The violent episodes themselves were
sporadic. At any given time they probably involved minor
percentages of the total population—certainly not more than
a small fraction of the number who were then engaging in
various sorts of group protest.

While it is probably true that protest by one or more
groups seeking to advance or defend its status in society has
been a continuous feature of American life, group violence has
not. Indeed, it is group protest, not group violence, that is as
American as cherry pie.

Do we have more group violence than other modern
nations? Comparisons with other countries are difficult. Our
Task Force Report shows a group violence casualty rate in
17 other industrially advanced nations for the first half of this
decade that is only one-fourth the United States rate.[4] (The
average for all nations, however, was 40 times the United
States rate.) Yet few advanced democratic nations are free
from group violence, as the riots in France, Germany, Italy,
Canada and Japan during the past two years and the continuing strife in Northern Ireland remind us. Unlike many
other countries (including some advanced ones), strife in the
United States is usually aimed at particular policies, conditions or groups rather than at overthrow of the government;
indeed, the United States has been free of anything resembling
insurrection for more than a century. Except for Great

---

[4] *Violence in America,* p. 448. This comparison is based on available
data that may not be fully comparable on a cross-national basis.

Britain, this country has the longest record of government continuity in the world.

Why does group violence occur in an advanced democratic society? We may accept that men naturally possess aggressive tendencies without concluding that group violence is inevitable. Nature provides us with the capacity for violence; material, social and political circumstances are the determinants of whether and how we exercise that capacity. Men's frustration over some of these circumstances is a necessary precondition of group protest. Whether that frustration will erupt into violence depends largely on the degree and consistency of social control and the extent to which social and political institutions afford peaceful alternatives for the redress of group grievances.

All societies generate some discontent because organized life by its very nature inhibits most human beings. Group violence occurs when expectations about rights and status are continually frustrated and when peaceful efforts to press these claims yield inadequate results. It also occurs when the claims of groups who feel disadvantaged are viewed as threats by other groups occupying a higher status in society. Greater expectations and frustrations for disadvantaged groups, and greater fears of threatened groups, are more likely to occur in times of rapid social change than in times of social stability.

America has always been a nation of rapid social change. We have proclaimed ourselves a modern promised land, and have brought millions of restless immigrants to our shores to partake in its fulfillment. Persistent demands by these groups —by the Western farmers of the revolutionary period, later by the Irish, the Italians and the Slavs, and more recently by Puerto Rican, Mexican, and Negro Americans—and resistance to these demands by other groups, have accounted for most of the offensive and defensive group violence that marks our history.

This analysis, however, does not adequately explain why some upper class and middle class students engage in group violence. Some affluent students doubtless perceive themselves as disadvantaged—by the draft and forced service in the Vietnam war, by their small voice in college governance, by their lack of identity and purpose in what they perceive as a complex, computerized and highly materialistic urban society. But for many students, the causes that attract them most are not their own grievances but those of the other groups and problems of the society as a whole. To a high degree, they are motivated by a sense of guilt for being privileged and by the desire of many young people to share with others in the experience of serving a noble cause. For most of those so motivated, participation in peaceful protest fulfills this need. Those few who are particularly impatient or cynical about the " system " or are committed to revolution resort to violence.

As we have noted, discontent is only one prerequisite of group violence. Whether violence actually occurs also depends on popular attitudes and how effectively political institutions respond to the threat of violence and to demands for the redress of group grievances. Although we have an open political and social system, more dedicated than most to the dream of individual and group advancement, the majority are sometimes unwilling either to hear or to redress the just grievances of particular minorities until violent advocacy or repression calls them to the forefront of our attention.

And for all our rhetoric to the contrary, we have never been a fully law-abiding nation. For example, some measure of public sympathy has often been with the night-riders who punished the transgressor of community mores and with the disadvantaged who sought to remedy obvious injustices by violent means. Lack of full respect for law and at least tacit support for violence in one's own interest have helped to make the United States, in the past as at present, somewhat more tumultuous than we would like it to be.

II.

The Rationale of Group Violence

Those who engage in group violence as a political tactic advance several reasons to support it. Some of the current justifications have been summarized by our Task Force on Violent Aspects of Protest and Confrontation.[5] They are stated as the militants themselves might make them.

1. Militants argue that the creation of turmoil and disorder can stimulate otherwise quiescent groups to take more forceful action in their own ways. Liberals may come to support radical demands while opposing their tactics; extreme tactics may shock moderates into self re-examination.

2. Militants point out that direct action is not intended to win particular reforms or to influence decision makers, but rather to bring out a repressive response from authorities—a response rarely seen by most white Americans. When confrontation brings violent official response, uncommitted elements of the public can see for themselves the true nature of the " system." Confrontation, therefore, is a means of political education.

3. Militants believe that if the movement really seriously threatens the power of political authorities, efforts to repress the movement through police-state measures are inevitable. The development of resistant attitudes and action toward the police at the present time is a necessary preparation for more serious resistance in the future.

4. Militants state that educated, middle-class, non-

---

[5] See *The Politics of Protest* (U.S. Government Printing Office: Washington, D.C., 1969), pp. 81-82.

violent styles of protest are poorly understood by working-class youth, black youth, and other "drop-outs." Contact with these other sectors of the youth population is essential and depends upon the adoption of a tough and aggressive stance to win respect from such youth.

5. Militants recognize that most middle-class students are shocked by aggressive or violent behavior. In the militant view, this cultural fear of violence is psychologically damaging and may be politically inhibiting. To be a serious revolutionary, they say, one must reject middle-class values, particularly deference toward authority. Militant confrontation gives resisters the experience of physically opposing institutional power, and it may force students to choose between "respectable" intellectual radicalism and serious commitment to revolution, violent or otherwise.

6. Militants respond to those who point to the possibility of repression as a reaction to confrontation tactics by accusing them of wishing to compromise demands and principles and dilute radicalism. Militants believe that repression will come in any case, and to diminish one's efforts in anticipation is to give up the game before it starts.

Somewhat different arguments are advanced by those among threatened groups to justify defensive private violence and the use of excessive force by public authorities. They believe that the disadvantaged group will cease to exert pressure only if protesters are firmly and decisively repressed and that strong evidence of superior force and willingness to use it will succeed in defending the status quo.

These arguments for group violence—offensive or defensive[6]

[6] We use the term "offensive" violence as violence used to advance the cause of a protesting group, and the term "defensive" violence as violence used to defend the position of the group threatened by protest. Occasionally, a peacefully protesting group met with defensive violence as so defined may engage in counter-violence as a means of self defense, as is true of the Negro Deacons for Defense in Mississippi and Alabama.

—are not sustained by history, contemporary reality, logic or law. They are inconsistent with the basic principles of democratic government.

We put to one side the efficacy of violence in overturning a government or maintaining it in power, for this has not been the main thrust of American group violence. The thornier question—one that is more pertinent to American practitioners of group violence who usually aim not at seizing or defending the government but at altering or continuing its policies—is whether group violence is an effective, albeit illegal, tactic for winning or preventing a significant change of status.

History provides no ready answer to this question. There have been a great many protest movements marked by violence which eventually achieved some of their aims. But whether offensive violence by the protesting group helped or hindered the subsequent achievement remains a matter of conjecture, as does the question of whether defensive violence by the threatened group hindered or helped the eventual change. In the history of the American labor movement, for example, violence persistently accompanied the struggle of workingmen to gain decent working conditions and recognition for their unions; both ends were eventually achieved, but there are differences of opinion whether pro-labor violence helped the cause or whether anti-labor violence hindered it.[7] Labor leaders themselves doubted the effectiveness of violence, and no major labor organization in American history advocated violence as a policy. Typically, pro-labor violence was a response to the use of excessive force by militia or private police or strikebreakers. While violence proved to be a better short-run weapon for employers than for workers, the escalation of counter-violence it produced was a factor in the

---

[7] In *Violence in America*, p. 290, Philip Taft and Philip Ross conclude: "The effect of labor violence was almost always harmful to the union. There is little evidence that violence succeeded in gaining advantages for strikers."

passage of the laws that eventually established the rights of labor.

It is no doubt true that in the 1960's policy changes advantageous to dissident groups have sometimes followed in the wake of urban riots and campus disturbances. These gains, however, may have been attributable more to the validity of the protest goals than to the violent outbreaks when they came. Moreover, to the extent violence may have contributed to these gains, the use of excessive force against peaceful demonstrators—as in Birmingham—may have been more decisive than any violence by the demonstrators themselves. No one will ever know whether as much or more might have been won without resort to violence by either side. The advocacy and practice of deliberate violence by some radical black militants and some student and anti-war activists have certainly created antagonism and resulted in the loss of sympathy for these causes among large sectors of the public. Leaders of many protesting groups recognize the counterproductivity of violence; before the November Peace Mobilization in Washington, many of the protest leaders sought diligently to discourage violence by such groups as the Weatherman faction and the Youth International Party. When these factions did resort to violence, leaders of the Mobilization expressly disavowed and condemned them.

If the lessons of history are ambiguous on the short-term effectiveness of violence as a political tactic, they are clear on its long-term dangers. As we noted in our Statement on Campus Disorder, violence tends to feed on itself, with one power group imposing its will on another until repressive elements succeed in reestablishing order. The violent cycles of the French and Russian Revolutions and the decade resulting in the Third Reich are dark abysses of history to ponder. Violence tends to become a style, with many eager followers. German students setting fire to cars in West Berlin chanted in English: " Burn, baby, burn." When students last year violently took control of the telephone system at Brandeis University, within ten days British, French, German and

Italian students attempted to do the same thing. Violently disruptive tactics that began inappropriately in universities have been copied even more inappropriately in high schools and churches.

As our Task Force on Law and Law Enforcement has found, the danger of this contagion is that extreme, unlawful tactics will replace normal legal processes as the usual way of pressing demands. Given present trends, it is not impossible to imagine an America in which the accepted method for getting a traffic light installed will be to disrupt traffic by blocking the intersection, where complaints against businessmen will call for massive sit-ins, where unsatisfactory refuse collection will cause protesting citizens to dump garbage in the street. We do not believe that a healthy society can result from the widespread use of such techniques.

As our Task Force concluded, group violence as a tactic to advance or restrain protest by discontented groups does not contribute to the emergence of a more liberal and humane society but produces an opposite tendency. The fears and resentments created by these tactics have strengthened the political power of some of the most destructive elements in American society.

As one of this nation's most thoughtful leaders has observed:

> No society can live in constant and destructive tumult. . . . The anarchist plays into the hands of the authoritarian. Those of us who find authoritarianism repugnant have a duty to speak out against all who destroy civil order. The time has come when the full weight of community opinion should be felt by those who break the peace or coerce through mob action.[8]

---

[8] John W. Gardner, *No Easy Victories* (New York: Harper and Row, 1968), p. 5.

III.

Elements of Prevention and Control

What steps should a representative constitutional society take to prevent and control group violence? Our political institutions should be so framed and managed as to make violence as a political tactic both unnecessary and unrewarding. To make violence an unnecessary tactic, our institutions must be capable of providing political and social justice for all who live under them and of correcting injustice against any group by peaceful and lawful means. To make violence an unrewarding tactic, our political and social institutions must be able to cope with violence when it occurs and to do so firmly, fairly, and within the law.

Our Constitution was written after the violent overthrow of a colonial government which followed one of these imperatives, but ignored the other. Its preamble does not speak merely of justice, or merely of order; it embraces both. Two of the six purposes set forth in the Preamble are to " establish justice " and to " insure domestic tranquility." The First Amendment sets forth a third and closely related goal—to protect the rights of free speech and peaceable assembly, and the right to petition the Government for redress of grievances. If we are to succeed in controlling group violence, we must navigate by all three of these stars.

History is full of violent disasters that occurred because channels for peaceful presentation of grievances were blocked and because governments did not or could not act to correct the underlying injustices or to control disorder; history also contains examples of disasters that were averted by governments which kept the channels of protest open and applied a judicious combination of reform and control.

The French and Russian Revolutions reached extraordinary peaks of violence because absolutist governments concentrated on efforts to restore order and refused to redress grievances or transfer a sufficient share of power to the emerging lower classes. The British, on the other hand, averted a similar disaster by judicious measures of control and by more flexible development of their political institutions to accommodate the rights and needs of all their people.[9] In Germany, after World War I, the Weimar Republic was too weak either to control street fighting between right wing and left wing students and workers or to remedy their grievances; the emergence of Hitler to " restore order " proved to be a disaster for the entire world.

In our own country, we have on some occasions failed to take the necessary measures of reform and control; on other occasions we have succeeded. We proved unable to abolish the injustice of Negro slavery without a bloody war—a conflict which released currents of violence that continue to flow a century later. The Reconstruction governments in the Southern states were too weak to enforce the newly won rights of black people against a hostile community or to prevent the Ku Klux Klan from reestablishing white supremacy by violence. The struggle of the labor unions was marked by extensive restrictions on peaceful protest and by repressive violence in the absence of laws to provide minimum standards of justice for working people and legal machinery for the resolution of disputes; the violence largely subsided after such laws were enacted. And in the wake of the Great Depression, after relatively few violent incidents such as the Bonus March and the farmers' defense of their lands against foreclosure, we averted further violence by fashioning major alterations in the rights of individuals to government assistance and in the responsibilities of government for directing the course of our private enterprise economy.

When group violence occurs, it must be put down by lawful means, including the use of whatever force may be required. But when it occurs—better still, before it occurs—we

[9] See B. C. Roberts, " On the Origins and Resolution of English Working Class Protest," in *Violence in America*, pp. 197-220.

must permit aggrieved groups to exercise their rights of protest and public presentation of grievances; we must have the perception to recognize injustices when they are called to our attention, and we must have the institutional flexibility to correct those injustices promptly.

We do not mean, of course, that the mere making of a demand entitles it to be granted, or that the particular remedy proposed by those aggrieved should be adopted. Some "non-negotiable" demands by students, by radical black militants, by anti-war demonstrators and others are unrealistic and unfair to the rights of others; some proposed remedies are self-defeating or administratively unworkable. What is essential is that when the basic justice of the underlying grievance is clear, an effort to take suitable measures of accommodation and correction must be made. The effort must be made even though other groups feel threatened by the proposed correction, and even though they may resort to violence to prevent it. We cannot "insure domestic tranquility" unless we "establish justice"—in a democratic society one is impossible without the other.

We therefore put forth our suggestions as to how these three goals—controlling disorder, keeping open the channels of protest, and correcting social injustices—can be more successfully pursued.

IV.

Strategies of Control

Many feel that rioters should be dealt with harshly. At least two-thirds of white Americans, according to one poll, believe that looters and fire-bombers should simply be shot down in the streets.[10] Many believe that even peaceful demon-

[10] See the Report of this Commission's Task Force on Law and Law Enforcement, *Law and Order Reconsidered* (U.S. Government Printing Office: Washington, D.C., 1969), p. 335.

strators are " agitators " or " anarchists." In a poll conducted
for this Commission, 56% agreed that " any man who insults
a policeman has no complaint if he gets roughed up in
return."

As recent history illustrates, the prompt, prudent deploy-
ment of well-trained law enforcement personnel can extin-
guish a civil disorder in its incipiency. But history also
demonstrates that excessive use of force is an unwise tactic for
handling disorder. To the generalization made earlier, that
violence is an always dangerous and sometimes ineffective
tactic for dissident groups pressing their demands or for
threatened groups resisting those demands, may be added this
corollary: the use of excessive and illegal force is an always
dangerous and usually ineffective tactic for authorities seeking to quell unrest. Both in the short and in the long run, the
use of excessive force to repress group violence often has the
effect of magnifying turmoil, not diminishing it.

It is useful to contrast the official response to the anti-war
protest in Chicago during the Democratic National Convention of 1968 and the " counter-inaugural " in Washington on
January 20, 1969. These two events were organized by many
of the same protesting groups and attended by many of the
same individuals, in roughly equal numbers. Yet the results of
these events were markedly different. In Chicago, the authorities were restrictive in granting demonstration permits; some
of the police, deliberately goaded by verbal and physical
attacks of small militant groups, responded with excessive
force not only against the provocateurs but also against peaceful demonstrators and passive bystanders. Their conduct,
while it won the support of the majority, polarized substantial
and previously neutral segments of the population against the
authorities and in favor of the demonstrators.[11]

---

[11] The ongoing Democratic Convention and the possible desire of some
demonstrators to influence its outcome by violence may have intensified
the disorder in Chicago—a circumstance absent during the Washington
Inaugural.

In Washington, demonstration permits were liberally issued. Although there was also provocative violence by some of the demonstrators, the police used only that force clearly necessary to maintain order. As a result, there was little criticism of police behavior. Our analysis leads to the conclusion that the amount of violence that occurred during these demonstrations and the resulting effects on public opinion were directly related to the kind of official response that greeted them.[12]

In both instances a small number—no more than a few hundred in either case—intended to provoke a " confrontation " with authorities by provocative acts, aimed especially at policemen. A majority of the participants intended to demonstrate peacefully and, in fact, did so.

In response to reports that violence and disruptive conduct would occur, Chicago authorities adopted tight, well-publicized security measures designed to dissuade protesters from coming to the city. To discourage the protesters further, they prolonged the negotiations for demonstration permits and exercised their discretionary powers restrictively. The limited, begrudging dialogue with protesting groups reduced the opportunity of the authorities to assess and separate the component groups in the demonstration (many of which intended to demonstrate peacefully) and to learn the details of their plans. This resistant posture served to discourage more mature and responsible protesters from coming while firing the determination of young militants to attend and confront. To some of the police and some Chicago citizens, the official posture of resistance signified that the protest activities as such were dangerous or illegitimate; they tended to view protesters as troublemakers and law-breakers, thus failing to discriminate between the small number of radicals seeking trouble and the great majority of peaceful citizens exercising their constitutional rights.

[12] The Washington authorities had also dealt successfully with the large-scale anti-war march on the Pentagon in October 1967, before the Chicago experience the following summer.

In preparation for the Inaugural in Washington five months later, intelligence reports were carefully evaluated. Genuine threats were sorted from theatric exaggerations. Troublemakers were identified and watched closely, but no attempt was made to interfere with the activities of the majority of peaceful demonstrators. Authorities negotiated conscientiously with protest leaders and arrived at agreements on the scope of permits for parades and meetings that were acceptable to all parties. The protest leaders, impressed with the reasonableness of the government spokesmen, made substantial efforts to cooperate with officials and ensure peace.

As the Chicago and Washington events differed in preparation, they differed in outcome. After minor skirmishes, trouble in Chicago escalated when throngs of demonstrators, having been denied permits to remain overnight, refused to leave Lincoln Park, their main gathering place. Dozens of police attempted to clear the park on three successive nights. In response to serious and deliberate provocations, but without coherent planning, some policemen clubbed and teargassed guilty and innocent alike, chasing demonstrators through streets some distance from the park. Particularly on the side streets, some bystanders who had taken no part in the demonstrations were attacked by police officers. Several media representatives were clubbed and had their cameras smashed. Predictably, tensions and anger rose. Extremists who would otherwise have been ignored began to attract audiences. They urged demonstrators to fight back. The police were exposed to more and more jeers and obscenities and had to withstand heavier barrages of rocks and other missiles. During one of the first nights, 15 policemen were injured; two nights later, 149 were injured.

In Washington, the cycle of escalating violence never got started. Both verbal and physical provocations by demonstrators were frequently intense, but they were met with restraint. Provocation by policemen was rare; when it occurred it was terminated by police and city officials who intervened quickly to restore discipline. In general, police withstood physical and verbal abuse with great calm. In the end, the behavior of Washington officials and the police won praise in newspaper editorials and from leaders of the demonstration.

There were some radical leaders, however, who were more grateful for the official response in Chicago, for it appeared to validate their characterizations of government as being " reactionary " and " repressive " and to increase support from other protesting groups. The chaos at Chicago also gave solidarity to the ranks of those who regard all demonstrators, however peaceful, as irresponsible " punks." The overall effect was to increase polarization and unrest, not diminish them.

This comparison between Chicago in August of 1968 and Washington January 1969 can be closed on two encouraging notes. Permits for peace marches in Chicago were sought and granted in October 1969. The marches were organized by the " Weatherman," an extremely militant faction of the Students for a Democratic Society. In the course of the demonstrations, Chicago police had to face four days of intense provocation and wanton violence. This time, however, the police acted with calm and restraint. No injuries to residents, bystanders or newsmen were reported; on the contrary, the police took steps to safeguard bystanders from the violence. As a result of the professional conduct of Chicago police, violence was effectively contained, and blame for the damage and injuries that did occur fell squarely upon the violent group among the demonstrators, many of whom were arrested.

The Peace Moratorium Parade and assembly in Washington on November 15 was another example of intelligent and restrained official response. Although the government had reason to expect that some elements among the protesting groups were bent on violence, reasonable permits were ultimately negotiated with the responsible demonstration leaders, and ample police and military force were provided to preserve order if necessary. In the largest single protest demonstration in American history, the overwhelming majority of the participants behaved peacefully. Their activities were facilitated rather than restrained by the police. When the few extremists did attempt violent attacks on two occasions, the police responded quickly and firmly but, on the whole, without excessive force.[13] As a result, order was maintained, the right to protest was upheld, and it was possible to judge both the peaceful and the violent aspects of the protest in their true proportion.

Civil governments must, of course, act promptly and decisively against threats to public order. As the National Advisory Commission on Civil Disorders stated: " Individuals cannot be permitted to endanger the public peace and safety, and public officials have a duty to make it clear that all just and necessary means to protect both will be used."[14]

A parallel duty exists for colleges and universities: they must have firm, well-publicized plans for dealing swiftly and decisively with campus disorders. The practice of keeping rules fuzzy so that dissident groups are " kept off balance " has failed demonstrably. In our Statement on Campus Disorders of June 1969, we recommended that students, faculty and administrators develop acceptable standards of conduct and responses appropriate to deviations from those standards, including the circumstances under which they will resort to i) campus disciplinary procedures, ii) campus police, iii) court injunctions, iv) other court sanctions, and v) the city police. We believe genuine progress is being made in this direction.

---

[13] The bulk of the actual work of maintaining the peacefulness of the proceedings was performed by the demonstrators themselves. An estimated five thousand " marshals," recruited from among the demonstrators, flanked the crowds throughout. Their effectiveness was shown when they succeeded in stopping an attempt by the fringe radicals to leave the line of march in an effort to reach the White House during the Saturday parade.

Fringe groups among the demonstrators, numbering approximately 100, provoked two confrontations by throwing rocks at police on Friday night, November 14, as they unlawfully attempted to march on the Embassy of South Vietnam, and again on Saturday evening when rocks and paint bombs were used during an otherwise lawful assembly at the Justice Department. On both occasions, police used tear gas to disperse the crowds among which the extremists were mingled.

[14] *Report of the National Advisory Commission on Civil Disorders* (U.S. Government Printing Office: Washington, D.C., 1968), p. 171.

Police manuals recognize that when the police are needed—as in urban riots, demonstrations that threaten violence, and campus disorders in which court injunctions must be enforced—their behavior must be calm and impartial, however intense the provocation. Panic, overt expression of anger, and inflammatory use of force are serious breaches of police discipline. The FBI riot control manual states that:

> The basic rule, when applying force, is to use only the minimum force necessary to effectively control the situation. Unwarranted application of force will incite the mob to further violence, as well as kindle seeds of resentment for police that, in turn, could cause a riot to recur.[15]

147527

The National Advisory Commission on Civil Disorders has provided excellent, detailed prescriptions for improving police practices, especially in handling urban riots.[16] Despite notable progress since the Commission issued its report in March 1968, many police departments in American cities are still ill-prepared to handle riots and other civil disorders.

In a survey of 16 major cities, this Commission's Task Force on Law and Law Enforcement found that few city governments had established formal, dependable communication links with dissident groups. Few had adequate plans for dealing with disorders, and effective planning staffs were rare. Though all have added riot control to the curriculum of police training, the number of hours devoted to training per man has not increased significantly.

We therefore urge police departments throughout the nation to improve their preparations for anticipating, preventing and controlling group disorders, and to that end to study the approaches that have been employed successfully on the three most recent occasions in Washington and Chicago.[17]

[15] *Law and Order Reconsidered*, p. 352.
[16] *Report*, Chapter 12.
[17] See generally, *Law and Order Reconsidered*, Chapters 15 and 16.

V.

Keeping Open the Channels of Peaceful Protest

We have pointed out the fundamental distinction between protest and violence, the fact that there is no necessary connection between them, and the need to vindicate the former while opposing the latter. As we have noted, the First Amendment to the Constitution protects freedom of speech, freedom of the press, and " the right of the people peaceably to assemble and to petition the Government for a redress of grievances." In the Supreme Court's words, the First Amendment entails a " profound national commitment to the principle that debate on public issues should be uninhibited, robust and wide open."[18]

Obstructions to peaceful speech and assembly—whether by public officials, policemen, or unruly mobs—abridge the fundamental right to free expression. On the other hand, speech, assembly and other forms of conduct that become coercive or intimidating invade the fundamental First Amendment rights of other citizens. When a mob forces a university to suspend classes, the rights of teachers to teach and students to learn are abridged; when a speaker is shouted down or forced from a platform, he is deprived of freedom to speak, and the great majority of the audience is deprived of freedom to listen.

Society's failure to afford full protection to the exercise of these rights is probably a major reason why protest sometimes results in violence. Although these rights are expressly safeguarded by the federal Constitution, the existing remedies available to aggrieved persons are not adequate. The only approximation to an effective remedy at the federal level is a court injunction authorized under 42 U.S.C. sec. 1983, a

[18] *New York Times vs. Sullivan*, 376 U.S. 254.

Reconstruction era civil rights statute that creates a private cause of action for the "deprivation of any rights, privileges, or immunities secured by the Constitution" by any person acting "under color of" state law. The relative ineffectiveness of this private remedy is indicated by the rarity with which injunctions have been sought in the thirty years since the statute was first interpreted to apply to interference with First Amendment rights. Moreover, state officials acting under color of state law are not alone in posing threats to First Amendment rights; on college campuses, for example, the protesters themselves have obstructed free speech and peaceful assembly. No present federal law affords a remedy for private abridgement of First Amendment rights.[19]

Accordingly, we recommend that the President seek legislation that would confer jurisdiction upon the United States District Courts to grant injunctions, upon the request of the Attorney General or private persons, against the threatened or actual interference by any person, whether or not under color of state or federal law, with the rights of individuals or groups to freedom of speech, freedom of the press, peaceful assembly and petition for redress of grievances.

Under present law private citizens can seek federal injunctions in instances where the complainant alleges unreasonable denial of permits for parades or meetings by state or federal officials or their issuance only on excessively restrictive conditions. Private persons can also obtain federal injunctive relief on proof of suppression by government agencies or their employees of publications or communications (including the seizure or destruction of newsmen's cameras or film) or the use by law enforcement officials of excessive or unauthorized force to arrest or disperse individuals who seek to make law-

[19] The Supreme Court has suggested that federal statutory remedies against such private acts of interference are constitutional, but that no statute yet enacted provides them. *United States v. Guest*, 383 U.S. 745.

ful expressions of their views. Our proposal would authorize the Attorney General, as well as private persons, to initiate such proceedings in appropriate cases involving state or federal action. It would also authorize suits for injunctions, both by the Attorney General and by private persons, against private obstruction of the exercise of free expression by pushing speakers off platforms, by the making of deliberately excessive noise, or by seizure of or denial of access to buildings or other facilities, streets and public areas—a type of interference with First Amendment rights not now covered by any federal statute.

The statute should also authorize suits for either damages or an injunction by the persons aggrieved and allow the Attorney General to intervene in such suits on request of the parties or the court or on his own motion. State and federal courts should be given concurrent jurisdiction to enforce the statute.

Our proposal suggests a greater federal role in preserving freedom of expression. We do so because federal district courts, which often deal with somewhat comparable provisions in other areas of federal law, are experienced in handling requests for injunctions expeditiously and fashioning careful and effective decrees. The use of federal court injunctions would also provide for greater uniformity in the judicial treatment of those infringing the constitutional rights of others. It would increase the likelihood that the experience of one community or institution would be readily available and useful in handling subsequent problems elsewhere.

State remedies against private misconduct involving infringement of First Amendment rights are usually based not on the First Amendment but on trespass statutes or disorderly conduct ordinances. Such laws were not written to deal with acts of physical obstruction, particularly those committed for demonstrative purposes, and are not always effective in handling such conduct. Moreover, where acts of violence or obstruction are committed in the name of righting fundamental grievances, those engaging in such conduct may find it harder to justify disobedience of court orders issued to uphold the First Amendment than would be true of orders based upon the laws against trespass and disorderly conduct. In recent legislation, Congress has given the Attorney General an increasingly active role in protecting certain vital individual rights. This approach seems particularly appropriate for the protection of First Amendment rights, since the mechanism of peaceful dispute, debate, compromise, and change is so essential to the preservation of a just and orderly society and since private persons are often unable to protect their First Amendment rights without some assistance.

For speech, petition and assembly to be effective, they must be heard and seen. In 1789 this was a regular consequence of exercising one's First Amendment rights. In today's crowded and complex society, however, being seen and heard depends almost entirely upon the printed and electronic news media, which are necessarily selective in picking out the relatively few items in a day's or a week's events that can be fitted into the space or time available for reporting "news." The *New York Times* daily receives 1.25 to 1.5 million words of news material from its correspondents and news services; of that amount, only about one-tenth is printed.

Moreover, the number of separate, independent news "voices" has not kept up with the growing size and diversity of the nation. Economic factors have forced down the number of regularly published daily newspapers and weekly magazines despite substantial population increases. The number of radio and television stations in any area is greater but still relatively small; more importantly, there is little difference among them in their reporting of the "news." Protesting groups can and do print their own newspapers and handbills, but their circulation is rarely extensive. All in all, the number of efforts to gain attention through the exercise of free speech and assembly far exceeds the number that impact upon the public consciousness as news. For example, the *New York Times* received over 37,000 letters to the editor last year; only 6% were published, though at least 85% were, in the words of the *Times* motto, considered "fit to print."

Had they all been printed, they would have completely filled 135 daily issues of the newspaper.

The difficulties presented by today's society for those who want their protests and demonstrations to be seen and heard leave most people unaware of how deeply felt many grievances have become. A decade ago it would have been fair to say—as many thoughtful journalists have since admitted— that the press did too little reporting of the existence of social injustice and of the grievances of protesting groups. It was generally thought that open conflict—especially violent conflict—was the most important kind of news. Too few news reports went beyond a description of "who-what-when-where" into the "why" of social and political analysis. The national press, for example, has acknowledged its past short-comings in covering the life and the problems of our black, Indian and Latin American minorities and their efforts to redress their grievances.

Today, in-depth analysis of underlying social conditions is now a regular and welcome part of the best of our print and broadcast media. Many responsible journalists now recognize more fully the challenge of their crucial role in creating the public understanding of complex modern problems that is a necessary pre-condition for informed democratic decisions on the timing and content of peaceful social and institutional change. Indeed, some critics—wrongly in our opinion—complain that the media now go too far in reporting protests and in commentary on their causes.

Like the Kerner Commission before us, this Commission has struggled with the question of what public or private measures a governmental body might recommend to improve the efforts of the press to report on the problems facing individuals and groups in American society and alternative means proposed for solving them, as well as on protest and its underlying causes. We have concluded that the indispensable element of a free press is pluralism and diversity: we need more effective and different voices, not fewer and fewer standardized or homogenized ones.

*Accordingly, we recommend that private and govern-
mental institutions encourage the developments of competing news media and discourage increased concentra-
tion of control over existing media.*

Apart from such strictly limited measures of government
intervention as the " fairness doctrine " for broadcasters who
operate under public licence—which deals not with the substance of broadcast speech but only with the broadcaster's
duty to present all sides—we oppose official attempts to
control how the media present and interpret the news. Governmental interference with the free press is no way to cure
its defects. The need is rather for constant self-appraisal and
for responsible, effective criticism of the media by private
entities such as university schools of journalism and by any
group or individual, public or private, aggrieved by any
aspect of media performance.

*We urge that the members of the journalism profession
continue to improve and re-evaluate their standards and
practices, and to strengthen their capacity for creative
self-criticism, along the lines suggested in the staff report
of our Media Task Force.*[20]

An observer of the current journalistic scene has recently
observed:

It ought to be plain, but seemingly it is not, that the
quality of journalism depends primarily on journalists—

[20] These suggestions include more attention to in-depth, interpretive
news reporting; hiring and training newsmen from minority groups and
providing equivalent regular coverage of minority group activities including births and deaths, business promotions and social functions, as
well as larger issues; and creation of vehicles for responsible criticism of
news media performance, including internal grievance machinery within
news organizations, community press councils, professional journalism
reviews, and a national center for media study. See *Mass Media and
Violence,* to be published.

not on government and not on the legal owners of
media . . .

Journalism will always need artistry to reach the
public's mind and heart. Indeed, what is now required is
a higher level of art, a boldness that will get journalism
unstuck from forms of communication developed in and
for a social context very different from the present.
Nobody except journalists can develop such forms.[21]

VI.

Establishing Justice

The third element in any program for reducing group
violence is to see to it that our political and social institutions
"establish justice" and that valid grievances of disadvantaged
groups of citizens are redressed in a timely manner.

Man's progress has reached a stage in which several forces
combine to create critical stresses in our social and political
structure. First, technological advances and population growth
have wrought profound and complex changes in our physical
environment and our ability to control it so as to meet basic
human needs. Second, an extended period of considerable
progress in raising standards of living and education for all
and in providing greater social justice for disadvantaged
groups—however unevenly—has created rising expectations
of still further progress and demands that it be brought about.
Third, our political and social institutions and the programs
they manage are not changing rapidly enough to keep up with
the speed of change in the environment they are intended to
control. Although we now have the technological and

[21] Max Ways, "What's Wrong with News? It Isn't New Enough,"
Fortune Magazine, October 1969.

economic capability of releasing all our citizens from poverty and social deprivation, we have not been willing or able to fashion the changes in our political institutions and public programs that will bring to the disadvantaged the liberation that is almost within their grasp. This combination of forces creates demands for change that are not being met, and leads to protests that sometimes result in group violence.

To appreciate the magnitude of these forces and the stresses that result, we need look back no further than the beginning of this century. In 1900, within the memory of men still alive, we were a nation of 75 million people, of whom less than 40% lived in metropolitan areas. We rode in carriages or trains. We communicated by mail and the printed word.

Today, within the same land space, we have almost tripled our number. Two-thirds of us live in urban concentrations. We motor at high speeds over a nation paved with freeways. We fly across and between the continents. We communicate by telephone, radio and television. Our resources and the demands we place upon them have increased enormously; so has our individual specialization of function and our dependence on one another for shelter and food, for personal safety, and even for the purity of the air we breathe.

But our political and social institutions and programs have not kept pace. We have achieved the phenomenal forward leap to the moon, but we have not managed the flow of traffic in New York. Most of us now live in metropolitan areas, but as noted in our statement on Violent Crime, we have made few, if any, advances in the art of governing the urban environment. We desire peace, but we are now engaged in the fourth war of this century. Science has shown us how to produce so much food that surpluses embarrass us economically, yet millions are hungry. We boast of our dedication to the concept that all men are created equal, yet inequality of opportunity remains our most persistent problem.

Despite our special penchant for economic and technological innovation, we tend like other peoples to resist political and social change. Thomas Jefferson noted this phenomenon and its relationship to violence. After a life-time of public service, he observed:

> I am certainly not an advocate for frequent and un-tried changes in laws and constitutions. . . . But I know also, that laws and institutions must go hand in hand with the progress of the human mind. As that becomes more developed, more enlightened, as new discoveries are made, new truths disclosed, and manners and opinions change with the change of circumstances, institu-tions must advance also and keep pace with the times. We might as well require a man to wear still the coat which fitted him when a boy, as civilized society to remain ever under the regimen of their barbarous ancestors. It is this preposterous idea which has lately deluged Europe in blood. Their monarchs, instead of wisely yielding to the gradual change of circumstances, of favoring pro-gressive accommodation to progressive improvement, have clung to old abuses, entrenched themselves behind steady habits, and obliged their subjects to seek through blood and violence rash and ruinous innovations, which, had they been referred to the peaceful deliberations and collected wisdom of the nation, would have been put into acceptable and salutary forms.[22]

We strongly urge all Americans to reflect upon Jefferson's observations, and their special relevance to the causes and prevention of group violence. Today, the pace of change has become far more rapid than when Jefferson wrote, and the need for adapting our institutions to the changing environ-ment has become greater still. Today, more than ever before, we need to strengthen and utilize our institutions for peace-ful redress of grievances and peaceful accommodation to the quickening pace of social change.[23]

---

[22] Letter to Samuel Kerchival, July 12, 1816. *Writings of Thomas Jefferson* (Lippincott, 1871), Vol. VII, p. 15.

[23] In other statements and in our Final Report, we present our recom-mendations for achieving this goal.